THE NEOPLATONISTS

Other translations and works of philosophy available from Kyle Cathie include

The Jewish Mystics - Rabbi Louis Jacobs
Tao Te Ching - Stephen Mitchell
The Book of Job - Stephen Mitchell
George Fox and the Children of the Light - Jonathan Fryer

THE NEOPLATONISTS

Translated and introduced by

JOHN GREGORY

KYLE CATHIE

TO

KAREN

First published 1991 in Great Britain by
Kyle Cathie Limited
3 Vincent Square London SW1P 2LX

ISBN 1 85626 022 4

A CIP catalogue record for this book is available from the British Library

Designed by Lorraine Abraham
Typeset by DP Photosetting
Printed and bound by Cox & Wyman Ltd, Reading

Contents

John Gregory was born in 1938 and took degrees in Classics at Cambridge University, Philosophy at London University and Applied Linguistics at Durham University. Since 1961 he has worked as a teacher and college lecturer.

He translated from the Latin extracts for *The Illustrated Bede* by John Marsden (Macmillan, 1989) and *The Illustrated Columcille* (Macmillan, 1991).

Preface

THE NEOPLATONISTS who appear in this selection of texts are the pagan philosophers, beginning with Plotinus, who gave a new direction to Platonic philosophy between the third and the sixth centuries of the Christian era. The word 'Neoplatonists' is modern, reflecting the work of discriminating between the original philosophy of Plato's dialogues and later schools of Platonism that has occupied scholars during the nineteenth and twentieth centuries. Previously, these philosophers were simply Platonists; they regarded themselves as the authentic interpreters of the Platonic tradition, and it was their version of Platonism that was to exercise deep and wide-ranging influence on the thought of future centuries.

Philosophically, the Neoplatonists continued the well-established practice of synthesising the thought of Plato with the other main schools of Greek philosophy; and they were themselves responsible for important innovations. The impact of their work on their own and succeeding ages, however, is due even more to its religious and moral idealism: to its conception of reality as spiritual activity or states of consciousness, and of the human soul as a voyager, fallen and encumbered by bodily existence, yet perfectible by a path of ascent to its divine origins. As such, the Neoplatonist movement held a unique appeal for the educated classes of the later Roman empire, peculiarly adapted to the temper of its own – and future – ages. The teaching of Plotinus, coinciding with a period of material decline and religious anxiety unparalleled under the Roman Empire, has been described as the climax of 'a series of attempts to meet the supreme religious need of the later Hellenistic period by somehow bridging the gulf between God and the soul; to construct, that is to say, within the framework of traditional Greek rationalism a scheme of salvation capable of comparison and rivalry with those offered by the mystery religions' (Dodds, 1963, p. xviii).

In their combination of a sophisticated philosophy with religious aspiration, the pagan Neoplatonists had only one serious rival - Christianity; and, anti-Christian though they were, it was the incorporation of their ideas into Christian theology that ensured their permanent influence on European culture.

In the present century the Neoplatonists have had the good fortune to attract the attention of scholars who combine great depth of learning with a breadth of cultural interest and sympathy. Those from whom I have especially tried to profit are listed in the Bibliography.

I owe a special debt of gratitude to Kyle Cathie for commissioning this book, and also to John Marsden for his continuing encouragement and helpful advice. I, of course, remain solely responsible for whatever errors and inadequacies it might contain.

JG

'Plotinus, the philosopher of our time'

LIFE AND WORK

'Plotinus, the philosopher of our time, seemed ashamed of being in a body.' So begins the biographical essay by his disciple Porphyry, with a phrase that at once captures the spirit of Plotinus' philosophy and seeks to explain his reticence about his origins. He is said to have been born in AD 204–5, but there is no reliable tradition concerning his ancestry or place of birth. He was wary of allowing his personality, rather than his philosophy, to become the focus of his followers' loyalty, refusing to sit for his portrait and keeping secret his date of birth. Only one fact of his early life was confided to close friends, that his infantile compulsion to suck his nurse's breast continued till the age of eight, finally surrendering to ridicule – a detail of curiously modern interest.

Plotinus began his serious study of philosophy when in his late twenties, at Alexandria, the cosmopolitan centre of learning where western and eastern cultural influences coincided, and where a variety of philosophical schools were flourishing. His teacher for eleven years, Ammonius, is a shadowy figure who wrote no books, but we know that Plotinus became well-read in the works of Plato, Aristotle and their later commentators, and was familiar with the writings of other major schools of philosophy, notably the Stoics. Outside philosophy, also, his numerous quotations from the poems of Homer and allusions to Greek myth confirm his cultural background as thoroughly Greek.

In his thirty-ninth year, hoping to make acquaintance with the philosophy of Persia and India, he joined a disastrous military campaign against the Persians led by the Emperor Gordian III (238–44 AD) and on its defeat escaped with difficulty to settle in Rome, where the rest of his life's work was done. No evidence exists that Plotinus ever engaged in systematic study of eastern mystical thought, and modern scholars, when discussing the sources of his ideas, have differed considerably in the importance they have attached to the possibility of oriental influence.

In Rome, he moved among the ruling class, highly honoured by the Emperor Gallienus (253–68 AD) and his wife Salonina, and his seminars were attended by senators; but he took no interest in politics, urging his followers to withdraw from public life and abandon worldly ambition. He once proposed to found a new city in southern Italy, named after Plato, where he could lead his students in retirement from the world to live by Plato's 'Laws', but the project was thwarted by the opposition of courtiers.

His practice of the private virtues was exemplary. Being of a gentle and accessible nature, he was often invited to arbitrate disputes, and many of the highest rank entrusted him with the guardianship of their children and property. Ascetic in his habits, he condemned the eating of flesh, and shunned the social life of the public baths.

At times, he was favoured with a mystical experience, the precious culmination of physical, moral and intellectual discipline, which he interpreted as the union of his highest self with the ultimate source and goal of all existence, the infinite One or Good. The ascent to the brink of this spiritual state, attained on four occasions during Porphyry's six years with him, is described by Plotinus in a unique autobiographical reference introducing one of his treatises (IV 8):

> Often I have woken to myself out of the body, become detached from all else and entered into myself; and I have seen beauty of surpassing greatness, and have felt assured that then especially I belonged to the higher reality, engaged in the noblest life and

> identified with the Divine; and there established, I have attained to that supreme actuality, setting myself above all else in the realm of Intellect. And after this repose in the Divine, descending from Intellect to reasoning, I am perplexed as to how my descent comes about, and how my soul has become embodied - a soul, though in the body, of such manifest excellence.

As much as his extensive use of the philosophical tradition, his reflection on the personal experience recorded here became the foundation of Plotinus' metaphysical system, his view of human nature, and his moral and religious teaching.

Plotinus taught in Rome for ten years before starting to publish his thought in writing. Although his philosophy purports to be the authentic interpretation of Platonism, he saw himself not as a scholar or historian of ideas, but as a philosopher, and his classes typically began with a reading from a commentator of his own era as a stimulus to discussion and the introduction of his own ideas.

His teaching was notable for the impassioned but informal manner of his exposition, and for his encouragement of discussion and respect for the contributions of his students, in preference to the strictly deductive presentation of a formal lecture. A personal recollection of Porphyry's (*Life*, ch. 13) is illustrative:

> For three days I questioned him about the relation of the soul to the body, and he continued to explain. A man called Thaumasius had come in, who said he wanted to hear a general account from him in the form of a set lecture, and that he had no patience with Porphyry's questions and answers. Plotinus replied, 'But unless we solve the problems raised by Porphyry's questions, we shall have nothing to say to put into the lecture.'

This combination of critical dialogue with emotional conviction and informality of exposition is reflected in his written treatises. Fifty-four in number, these were occasional pieces composed in response to problems raised in the seminar, and originally circulated among a small group of carefully chosen students. Plotinus' entire philosophy, fully developed before he began to write them, is assumed throughout, and the major ideas keep recurring. Modern scholars have had very limited success in detecting signs of development between the earlier and the later works. Plotinus wrote rapidly and continuously, never pausing to revise, and even contemporaries sometimes found his words difficult to follow. The eminent scholar Longinus (213–72 AD), who honoured Plotinus for the scope and originality of his thought, once complained that copies of treatises sent to him were too full of scribal errors to be useful; but Porphyry assures us that they were faithful copies of the original, and that 'he did not understand the author's customary manner of exposition'.

During his last years Plotinus suffered a long and disfiguring illness, perhaps leprosy, and died in retirement from Rome at the age of sixty-six. His final words were a summary of his life's teaching:

> Strive to lead back the god within you to the Divine in the universe.

He owes his immortality to the publication of his treatises, thirty years after his death, by Porphyry, who edited them in six sets of nine (*Enneads*), an arrangement of his own, based roughly on their contents, which sometimes disrupts an original continuity of argument. Fortunately, he preserves the chronological order of composition in his essay *On the Life of Plotinus and the Order of his Books.* Problems of interpretation remain.

THE PHILOSOPHICAL CONTEXT

Plotinus drew extensively on a Greek philosophical tradition that stretched back to the sixth century BC. He disclaimed originality, professing to be no more than an interpreter of ancient philosophy, particularly the thought of Plato.

The philosophers before Plato, the Presocratics, were concerned chiefly with cosmogony; they sought to discover order, reason and simplicity in the universe by deriving the variety of phenomena from a single principle or set of principles, conceived of in materialist, or quasi-materialist, terms. Fruitful hypotheses were to find their way into later, more sophisticated philosophy, including Neoplatonism. The theory of Mind (*Nous*) as the moving cause of the material universe, from which it remains separate, was originated by Anaxagoras in the fifth century BC. Even earlier, Heraclitus had proposed a structural principle, or *Logos*, which maintains a rational equilibrium in the universe by balancing opposing forces. He also made a most significant connection between the exploration of the external world and the exploration of the self: the Logos is also in the soul of each of us, and to understand the world is to understand the self, and the key to right conduct.

In the work of Parmenides, also of the fifth century BC, we find the important rejection of the evidence of the senses and ordinary language as means to understanding the nature of reality. Contradictions are inherent in description of the phenomenal world, and the truth must be divined by reason (Logos): the true

Being which thought can entertain without contradiction must be One, without diversity or change, a complete, homogeneous and timeless sphere.

In these notions of Nous, Logos and the One, we see early Greek philosophy gradually feeling its way towards the concept of incorporeal existence. This is equally true of the early Pythagorean principle of Number, and their theory that the mathematical structure of the world was generated by a pair of primal and opposed elements, Odd and Even, or Limit and Unlimit - which entered Platonic and Aristotelian metaphysics as Form and Matter. Platonism, and later Neoplatonism, was also indebted to the Pythagoreans for the religious doctrines of the immortality and transmigration of the soul, and the kinship of all living things; and for the doctrine of inner purification through the contemplation of the underlying order of existence. It was Pythagoras himself who is said to have compared life to a festival, at which slavish men come to compete for fame or profit, but the best people attend as spectators.

Today the philosophy of Plato (c. 429–347 BC) is seen not as a complete and self-consistent system, but rather as an on-going process of exploration and self-criticism. Three major periods of Plato's thought have been identified: the early 'Socratic' dialogues, reflecting the method of the historical Socrates, in which the aim is to examine concepts, question presuppositions, and induce philosophical perplexity especially in the field of ethics; a middle period of constructive metaphysics; and a later critical period in which Plato subjects his idealist construction to close logical scrutiny and begins new lines of development.

This developmental perspective was unknown to the Neoplatonists, who treat Plato's thought as a unified whole, occasionally obscure but never really inconsistent. Not only the *Dialogues*, but Plato's *Letters*, now judged to be of doubtful provenance, and a late and famous lecture on the Good, known to us by report, were authoritative texts. The aspects of Plato's thought that most influenced them were his conception of the soul, his distinction between intelligible and sensible existence, his allusions to a single, transcendent Principle, and his account of the creation of the universe. These doctrines they found especially in books 6 and 7 of the *Republic*, in the *Phaedo*, the *Phaedrus*, the *Symposium*, the *Parmenides* and the *Timaeus*.

The soul, in Plato, is the source of life and movement, and is an incorporeal substance; it is also a person's true self, intellectual and moral, and immortal, the body being only a temporary habitation. In the *Phaedo* he presents a negative view of body as the soul's 'tomb', of the need for soul to despise and master bodily passions, and of the danger of 'drunken confusion' caused by sense-perception. The aim here is to escape from body. Elsewhere, soul is portrayed more comprehensively as tripartite – the reason, independent of body, together with emotions and appetites; and virtue is defined as the right functioning and relation of the parts, with reason in command.

In its disembodied existence, the rational part of soul has direct acquaintance with an intelligible realm of abstract Forms or Ideas, possessing substantial, independent and eternal Being, to which the formal properties of sensible existents stand as images to archetypes, and effects to their causes. Originally, a Form was supposed to be simple – nothing but itself, and a perfect instance of itself: Beauty is beautiful in perfection, all other beauties imperfect copies of it. But Plato later saw this to be inadequate: any form must interrelate with other forms – Beauty is Good, Same, Other, etc.; and does not the theory require a further Form of Beauty – 'a third man' – to explain the resemblance between Beauty and particular beauties, resulting in an infinite regress?

In the *Republic*, the form of Good has priority over all other forms. In the myth of the Cave, it is the Sun, which illuminates the world of real Being for the philosopher escaped from the shadows, and once the Good is described as '*beyond Being*' (509 b9); but it is still a form, and therefore finite and limited. In his late lecture, Plato identified the Good with Unity, and derived all other existence from it in conjunction with an opposite principle, the origin of plurality, called the *Indefinite Dyad* - apparently a new departure in his thought.

Of special significance for Neoplatonists was the *Parmenides*, in the second part of which the historical Parmenides is asked to examine the logical implications of his theory of the One, and proceeds to draw incompatible sets of conclusions both from the hypothesis that One exists and from its contradictory. In his first two arguments he demonstrates that the One must be without parts, boundless, formless, nowhere, timeless, without any attributes, and non-existent; and then, that the contrary conclusions must be true (Plato, *Parmenides*, 137–55). These and the following arguments, probably intended by Plato as criticism of his original ideal theory, using Unity as an example, were taken by the Neoplatonists as confirmation of the truth of their three hypostases of the ineffable and infinite One, the one-in-many of Intellect and the one-and-many of Soul.

Platonic education, the progress of the mind from sensible particulars to formal and abstract truths, culminates in the science of Dialectic, the study of intelligible Being. Forms are designed and classified in a hierarchy of ascending generality, differentiated but interdependent; at the summit stands the Good, the cause on which all others depend, and beneath it forms of great generality, activities of Being which are included in all more specific forms - the 'greatest kinds' which Plato's 'Sophist' exemplifies by Motion, Rest, Sameness and Otherness (254b *ff*).

In the story of creation in the *Timaeus*, the divine Artificer is represented as looking to the Forms as a model, and creating the material world by imposing forms upon Chaos, the pre-existing substrate, which resists perfect formation and is called a 'disorderly receptacle' (49 *ff*). This incorporeal matter, defined as 'space, not admitting destruction, apprehensible not by perception but by a kind of bastard reasoning, scarcely credible', reappears in Plotinus' negative conception of matter. The world created by Intellect is a living being, animated by the World Soul and individual souls, the self-moving causes of all life and motion.

It became a subject of controversy whether Plato intended to suggest that the world had a beginning, or was using the language of temporal process figuratively. In Plotinus, there is no moment of creation, and the picture of deliberation and planning is emphatically denied. But the *Timaeus* is his inspiration for that very positive valuation of the visible universe which stands alongside and in contrast to his ascetic rejection; and the orthodox doctrine of later Platonists, that the Ideas are the thoughts of God, is an interpretation of this dialogue that went to inform Plotinus' conception of Intellect. 'God wished all things to be good, and as far as possible without blemish . . . and so brought order out of disorder.' (30a)

Plotinus gives no systematic commentary on Plato, but rather comes to him for support after elaborating his own ideas. He has his favourite quotations, sometimes forced out of their original context. As with his other sources, his attitude to Plato is that of a philosopher, not a commentator or scholar. 'Plotinus' major motive for philosophising is to rationalise his own intuitions and experiences. Plotinus is a Platonist because Plato enables him to achieve this with the most success' (Rist, 1967, p. 185). The work of Plato was a supreme creative achievement which has dominated the history of Western philosophy; it was to receive a highly personal interpretation in the thought of Plotinus, and a new elaboration in the scholastic commentaries of the later Neoplatonists.

After the death of Plato, the Academy continued to flourish in Athens, and there were teachers of Platonism in other centres of learning like Alexandria. In the period known as Middle Platonism, which intervened between the Old Academy and the Neoplatonists, Plato's thought was preserved and developed with varying emphases. The important doctrine that the Forms are the thoughts of God became generally accepted. An eclectic approach was usual, seeking to reconcile Plato with Aristotelian, Stoic and Neopythagorean doctrines in particular. Also in vogue was philosophical scepticism, taught in the Academy until the first century of the Christian era, and continuing in its influence long after that. By concentrating on the 'Socratic' dialogues and Plato's arguments against the possibility of knowledge by sense-perception, it could be maintained that the true Platonism taught the impossibility of knowledge and the necessity of withholding judgement regarding ultimate reality. The grounds for doubt became formalised, and by the third century AD the case for Scepticism had been set out in detail by Sextus Empiricus. St Augustine refers to this 'despair of the truth' as a philosophical fashion of his own time (*Letter* Ia).

The characteristic mood of the *Enneads*, by contrast, is one of certainty; Plotinus regularly insists that his doctrines *must* be true, because reason demands it, and so sure is he that he often presupposes, rather than justifies, the premises from which his conclusions are drawn. It is likely that a reaction against Scepticism was one of the motivating forces behind Neoplatonism.

Of Aristotle, there is much critical discussion in the *Enneads* and also much adaptation of Aristotelian ideas. Aristotle's God, the Unmoved Mover who thinks only himself but moves the universe as the object of its love, influenced in different ways Plotinus' conception of the Good and his doctrine that the thinking Intellect is identical with intelligible beings.

To the 'third man' objection to Platonic Forms, the Neoplatonist answer is that Beauty and its images are not beautiful *in the same sense*: Beauty may be interpreted as an ordered series, of which the primary term, absolute Beauty, is participated in decreasing degrees by the others, at different stages of descent. The source of this idea is Aristotle, who calls the primary form of such a series '*universal, inasmuch as first*' (quoted in Lloyd, 1990, and described as 'an epigram which could serve as the motto of Neoplatonism', p. 78).

This concept pervades Neoplatonist thought: unity, good, being, life, soul, knowledge and virtue are all explained as having a range of meanings according to the level of existence at which they are found and their distance from the primal form.

In ethics, the Neoplatonists followed, but re-interpreted, Aristotle's distinction between two levels of virtue - called by Aristotle 'theoretical' and 'practical' - and his identification of happiness with the pursuit of the Good, particularly through the life of contemplation.

Porphyry tells us (*Life*, ch. 14) that in Plotinus' writings not only Peripatetic but also Stoic doctrines lie concealed. During the late Republican and early Imperial periods, it was Stoicism, more than any other school of philosophy, which had provided many educated Romans with an ethical ideal of life, and had inspired some in public life to choose suicide in preference to betrayal of principle. The survival of Stoic doctrines was ensured by the eclecticism of the later Empire, but as a separate school it gradually faded away. Its austere and rationalist ethic of duty and its materialism were perhaps out of tune with the religious temper of the times.

While rejecting the pantheism and materialism of the Stoics, and the determinism implied in their identification of Providence and Fate, Plotinus is strongly influenced by their moral philosophy, especially their teaching that virtue is the only good and that external circumstances are indifferent to the happiness of the wise man. Virtue, for the Stoics, was to know and live in harmony with the divine principle of Reason - or Logos - which governs the universe, and of which human reason is itself a manifestation. The Logos, imagined as a divine Fire, holds the universe itself in a single harmony.

It is curious that in the *Enneads* Plotinus refers to no philosopher later than the third century BC, although in his seminar the authors discussed were much closer to his own time. Two only of these will be mentioned here.

The work of Alexander Aphrodisias, head of the Peripatetic school in Athens at the start of the third century AD, is a fusion of the Platonic and Aristotelian traditions. He distinguished between two kinds of intelligible form, one immanent in matter and one transcendent, and two intellects, passive and active. Whereas immanent forms are known when the mind abstracts them from sense-data, transcendent forms are known eternally by the active intellect which is extrinsic to the individual man and identical with the divine Intellect. This may be Plotinus' immediate source for his doctrines that intelligible beings are identical with Intellect, and that in man intellect is unceasingly active in contemplation, even when we are unaware of it.

The philosopher whom Plotinus was specifically accused of plagiarising was Numenius of Apamea, usually labelled a Pythagorean – even while no sharp distinction existed between later Platonists and Pythagoreans. He represents the tendency to eliminate the ultimate dualism of One and Indefinite Dyad, or Limit and Unlimit, by the hypothesis of a single creative principle transcending both – an anticipation of the Plotinian One. He taught of a First God or Intellect, beyond Being and Form, the unmoving Cause of the universe, and of a second, active Intellect, which divides into second and third gods, the creators of the universe; each member of this trinity is present in man. He also taught that the whole of intelligible Being is contained in each of its parts, and that the creative Principle of the universe is not diminished by its effects – just as a teacher's knowledge is not diminished by being imparted to his pupils. Though on various points he differs from Plotinus, the resemblances are very striking; even Plotinus' best-remembered phrase, 'the solitary to the Solitary', is used by Numenius of man's contact with God.

This outline is sufficient to show how heavily indebted Plotinus was to the philosophic tradition. Although there are important original insights in his work, his impact is not to be explained by these, but rather by his special blend of rationalist metaphysics with religious experience and exploration of the self, a synthesis that matched the mood of his age.

PLOTINUS' SYSTEM OF THOUGHT

Plotinus was assured by personal experience that the individual human being is a microcosm of the universe. The true self, identified with the rational soul, is akin to the great Soul of the World, the Logos which creates and orders the visible universe by mediating intelligible forms to the substrate of Matter. Just as reason in the individual is informed by truths self-evident to intellect, the highest activity of mind, so the World Soul in its highest phase eternally contemplates the intelligible Forms that are the thoughts of universal Intellect. The material universe, like the body, is made as a faded image of the Intelligible, and a thing of temporal process: reality, or true Being, consists of states of consciousness, a hierarchy of spiritual activity, and is eternal.

At the still centre of the soul, man can attain to union with the infinite Principle of all creation, the Wellspring that engenders the whole sum of existence, and to which all that exists longs to revert. He, as absolute and self-sufficient simplicity, is called the One, and also, as the goal to which all things aspire, the Good. He may be called Power, Will, Beauty, even Love; but strictly, he is beyond knowledge, thought and description, without attributes, and beyond even existence, in the sense in which existence implies a determinate essence.

The One, Intellect and Soul, then, are the three transcendent sources – or hypostases – of existence. Creation is an eternal and spontaneous process: from the One proceeds Intellect, from Intellect Soul, and from Soul – in its lower phase, or Nature – the material universe, which is everlasting. Each hypostasis is undiminished by the giving of its power, and a trace of each is immanent in every level of creation. While the One remains, self-contented, both Intellect and Soul revert to contemplate their prior reality, and from their contemplation there issues eternally an overflow of creative energy. Everything that lives is contemplative according to its nature; even plants and rocks within the earth aspire to their Source. The whole universe is a single living organism, all its parts linked by a spiritual harmony and sympathy.

In the creative procession, the absolute simplicity of the One is manifested in ever-increasing multiplicity: the one-in-many of the forms in Intellect, the one-and-many of Soul, and the fragmented world of material bodies. The tendency to multiplicity is both a necessary expression of the primal Power and a falling away from the perfection that is Unity. When Plotinus distinguishes between higher and lower, or earlier and later, stages of creation, the reference is always to degrees of reality and perfection.

At the expiry of the creative energy is Matter, mere potentiality for reflecting forms, utter privation of Being, incorporeal and without qualities. Though a necessary substrate of the visible universe, by its very negativity and resistance to Form it functions within the metaphysical system as the source of Evil.

Within this system, Man is amphibious, his higher, disembodied soul in eternal contact with the Intelligible, its lower phase attached to body; and he can choose at which level to concentrate his attention and energy. To be absorbed in the individual body and its desires and sensations is to choose isolation from the Good and corruption by Matter, the source of all vice and evil. To rise to the level of reason, and then of intellect, is to re-discover one's origins in the unity of Being. To live in intellectual contemplation is the good for Man, and the only true Happiness, to which the body and material circumstances are irrelevant; it is an escape from temporal process into eternity.

The process of ascent or return is an inward movement into the depths of oneself, a spiritual progress by which the soul is gradually purified of all its bodily associations. The task of philosophy is to point the way. The first step is to recognise one's kinship with universal Soul; then, to learn to see intelligible form, reflecting the light of the Good, through the medium of physical beauty, of virtuous character and noble institutions, and of the abstractions of the sciences. The highest activity in this aesthetic, moral and intellectual training is Platonic dialectic, the science which divides and classifies the forms of Being. Within this life, the sage who attains to the contemplative state will necessarily continue to satisfy bodily needs, but as if for some other man not himself; he will practise indifference to the body, not mortification or extreme asceticism.

But dialectic studies the intelligible world from without, as an observer. By a further step in the ascent, the soul becomes Intellect and lives its riches from within, a mystical experience that Plotinus describes in almost surrealist language.

The ultimate reward of the contemplative life, union between the innermost soul and the Good which is the ground of all existence, is an experience to be waited for, a gift beyond the human will to command; it is an experience, not of excitement, but of stillness and utter simplicity, the soul being finally divested not only of all material accretions, but also of the rich diversity of the life of intellect. A favourite image by which Plotinus captures the unique intimacy of contact between the innermost self and the first Principle is that of concentric circles, representing the degrees of Being proceeding from the One; each has its own centre, but the centres coincide. To the attainment of the mystical state there is no easy short-cut, whether through secret knowledge, ritual observance, collective hysteria, or physical exercises; it is an experience reserved for the disciplined life of the sage, and therefore beyond the reach of the mass of mankind.

The unification of the soul on its inward progress is a solitary experience. There is no political dimension to the life of the sage, for Plotinus disparages the life of action as a poor substitute for contemplation, the best option for those unable to sustain the life of intellect. Even the practice of the social virtues is valued for its contribution to inner purification, not as the fulfilment of individual responsibility to the community. The aim is to escape from the world, not to engage with it. There could hardly be a sharper contrast with Plato's philosophers, after their escape from the Cave to behold the Sun, sent back into the Cave: for Plato, knowledge of the Good is the basis not only of private virtue, but also of the law and public policy, and the duty of the philosophers to apply their wisdom to the government of the state as shepherds of the people.

To this private pursuit of perfection, only the activity of teaching is a real exception. Perfection being always a creative and outflowing state, the sage will necessarily desire to impart his wisdom, and to share the thoughts of others travelling the same road.

In comparison with the Christian faith, the religion of Plotinus is individualistic, intellectual and elitist. In its view of Man and his relation to his Creator, there is also an optimistic humanism that contrasts with the Christian ideas of Man's sinful inadequacy and dependence on divine grace. Plotinian Man contains perfection always within himself, and can turn back to identify with it by his own efforts. There is no place for prayer or sacraments, nor does the Good care about its creation; although always present, it does not reach out to save.

THE HISTORICAL CONTEXT

The philosophy of Plotinus emerged out of critical engagement with the philosophical tradition that he inherited, and his inner experience; it cannot be treated as a by-product of external circumstances. But in accounting for the appeal which his thought held for its adherents, it is legitimate to look beyond philosophy. What did they find in Neoplatonism that answered human needs in the conditions of the later Roman Empire?

The third century AD was a period of unprecedented disaster for the Roman world, an age of foreign invasions and military defeat at the frontiers, of regular civil strife, and of economic crisis and widespread social unrest. During the time of Plotinus' residence in Rome, in particular, Gibbon tells us that 'there elapsed twenty years of shame and misfortune. During that calamitous period, every instant of time was marked, every province of the Roman world was afflicted, by barbarous invaders and military tyrants, and the ruined empire seemed to approach the last and fatal moment of its dissolution.' (Vol. I, p. 237). And through all this, the ruling classes of Rome, the cities and towns of Italy and the provinces experienced a new political impotence and want of purpose.

In the mid-century, three major wars were waged against the Persians in defence of the frontier on the Euphrates, campaigns which saw the death of one emperor, Gordian III, and the capture of another, Valerian, held prisoner until his death. Gallienus (AD 253–68), who ruled jointly with Valerian and succeeded him as sole emperor, also suffered the loss of all Rome's eastern provinces to the rebel city of Palmyra.

During the same years the Rhine–Danube frontier was repeatedly breached by northern invaders. The emperor Decius was killed in battle with the Goths in 251, and their retreat was secured by his successor only on the promise of annual tribute. Despite which, the Goths returned by sea to penetrate Pontus and Asia Minor, and occupy Greece, with widespread destruction and pillage. Marauding Franks overran Gaul and Spain, crossing to North Africa, and the Alemanni invaded Italy as far as Ravenna.

In the western empire, coinciding with the loss of the eastern provinces, a Roman governor, Postumus, declared independence from Rome, and for fourteen years controlled Gaul, Spain and Britain as a breakaway state.

Civil war between rival claimants for the imperial title became the norm, and the distinction between rightful emperor and pretenders was rendered meaningless. In the single year 238, Gordian was sole survivor of seven Caesars, and Rome itself the scene of bloody conflict between the Praetorian guard and forces loyal to the Senate. But it was rarely the Roman Senate that made the choice of emperor, new 'Caesars' being normally proclaimed by frontier legions on the battlefield. In this respect, as in others, the chaos was at its worst under Gallienus, the friend and admirer of Plotinus, when Gibbon lists nineteen alternative aspirants to the throne, all of whom met violent deaths, and the city of Alexandria laboured for years under the strife of rival factions. 'All intercourse was cut off between the several quarters of the afflicted city, every street was polluted with blood, every building of strength converted into a citadel; nor did the tumults subside till a considerable part of Alexandria was irretrievably ruined.' (Gibbon, op.cit. p. 280)

Foreign warfare put the Empire's financial resources under grievous strain, and throughout the third century an annual military tax, payable in kind and additional to regular land and poll taxes, was imposed on the peoples of the provinces. Many fled their homes to escape the exactions, and there survive pathetic letters of appeal, addressed to the emperors by desperate communities, against harassment by military and civilian officials and imperial agents. Debasement of the coinage and its issue in increasing quantities were practised by successive emperors; the age knew all the misery of galloping inflation, as prices rose in mid-century by almost 1,000 per cent in less than twenty years, and once-prosperous urban societies faced ruin. In the countryside manorial estates developed, absorbing smaller holdings and attracting tenants from the towns; they aimed at self-sufficiency and offered security in return for progressive serfdom.

It was a period of technical stagnation in both agriculture and industry, with a sharp social division between the owners of land, disdainful of manual labour, and a slave workforce with no incentive to improve its methods. Historians have observed a centrifugal tendency in the economy, by which industrial production was most vigorous in the frontier provinces and the centres that served the legions, in contrast with the urban decay of the older empire. Italy, in particular, became largely parasitic upon the rest of the empire, but the population of Rome, supported by free doles of food, knew the full horrors of the times only by report. Even Rome, however, was not spared the great plague which raged throughout the Empire between 250 and 265.

In central government, the Roman Senate had lost to the legions its power to appoint emperors, and to the emperor the determination of public policy and the making of law; and its members were drawn on less and less to fill provincial and military commands. Though retaining the wealth and some of the status of earlier times, their responsibilities were confined largely to administration and justice within Italy. Outside Rome, the powers of local magistrates and their councils were reduced to little more than the collection of taxes for the central government; civic office, once a matter for pride, became so unpopular that under Diocletian (AD 284–305) it was made an hereditary duty, enforced by law. The cities and towns lost their autonomy, both legislative and administrative, as control of the Empire's economy became increasingly centralised through imperial decrees, executed by the imperial civil service, and under the surveillance of imperial spies.

The Augustan concept of Principate, of a First Citizen in partnership with Senate and elected magistrates, had surrendered to an absolute autocracy. The official title of the emperor was now *Dominus*, or Lord, and emperors proclaimed their special relationship with divinity during their lifetime. A revival of military fortune under the successors of Gallienus had recovered the lost provinces and restored the frontiers, and the almost miraculous salvation of the State was their chief claim to glory. The outward trappings of dress - the jewelled diadem and gold-embroidered robe - reflected the shift towards monarchy, and from Domitian onwards the style of the imperial court was that of an oriental king. He rarely appeared in public, hedged about by a hierarchy of palace officials, and access was difficult; those privileged to be granted an audience were required to prostrate themselves, and the word 'sacred' became the standard epithet for imperial property and functions. In later Neoplatonism, the numerous orders of gods dependent on the One have been seen as metaphysical endorsement to the structure of imperial government.

THE RELIGIOUS CONTEXT

The birth of Neoplatonism coincides with that period of the Roman Empire 'when the material decline was steepest and the ferment of new religious feelings most intense'. (Dodds, 1965, p. 3)

The fear, sense of helplessness and alienation that were experienced throughout society in the conditions of the third century were not to find relief in the public worship of the Olympian gods, even though the emperors of the period continued to exploit the propaganda value of the divine protectors of the Roman State. The popular cult of the Sun, an important symbol for the Neoplatonists, shows the appeal of monotheism and the felt need for contact with a transcendent principle of life, which is also, through the mediation of its light and warmth, in intimate relationship with man.

For long before this time, certain eastern cults had been well established in Rome and the western provinces, and given official approval. The worship of Cybele, with its great nature drama of the death and rebirth of Attis, and its purificatory bathing in the blood of a bull or ram; and of Isis, Sarapis and Osiris, objects of daily devotion conducted by professional clergy in their temple complexes – such religions offered a colourful mythology and ritual with greater appeal to universal human emotions, membership of a supportive and privileged community, the possibility of personal relationship with a sympathetic deity, and the hope of immortality for faithful initiates into the mysteries.

The ancient Greek mysteries of Demeter and Persephone at Eleusis were similarly patronised by Roman emperors.

Under the Empire, a new wave of oriental beliefs and practices spread westwards. The cult of Mithras, Persian god of Light, which was restricted to men, was popular among the frontier legions and in the great commercial centres. The god, closely associated with the Sun, functioned as creator of the world, symbol of fertility, and protector of believers; his initiates attended regular sacred meals at which the god's life was enacted. The triumph of Good over Evil, represented in Mithras' slaying of the bull and eventual assumption into heaven on the Sun's chariot, addressed itself to a deep concern characteristic of the later Empire, the reality of evil in a divinely governed universe.

The various strands of thought known as Gnosticism combined elaborate creation mythologies with the doctrines that the material universe is inherently evil, an aberration from the original divine purpose, and that salvation, for an elect minority of mankind, comes by way of gnosis, a special, esoteric knowledge of the mysteries of creation. A Gnostic sect was established in Rome before the third century, including the Egyptian teacher Valentinus, whose particular version of Gnosticism appears to be the chief target of Plotinus' criticism in his treatise *Against the Gnostics* (II. 9). We are told in this work (ch. 10) that some of Plotinus' own associates continued to hold Gnostic beliefs even after joining him, and that he had failed to convert them. Gnostic ideas and early Christian theology were closely intertwined. Valentinian Gnosticism incorporates Christian concepts, and the Pauline epistles contain traces of the extreme dualism that judges the world and flesh to be wholly evil, and of the doctrine of redemption for an elect few.

In the fourth century, Manichaeism, a developed form of Gnosticism founded by Mani, a Babylonian contemporary of Plotinus, was to sweep westwards across the Roman Empire, claiming St Augustine among its adherents. It too preached a dualistic doctrine of precosmic forces of Light and Darkness at war in the universe, and the possibility of salvation for the Elect through worldly renunciation and asceticism. Widely popular, it was proscribed by the later Emperors and attacked by both Neoplatonist and Christian writers.

The uncertainties of the third century led many, at all levels of society, to look for guidance in astrology. That the stars were gods was generally accepted in the ancient world, even by the most sophisticated philosophers, and it was widely held that the harmonious order of the universe, linking earthly with celestial phenomena, permitted prediction in all areas of human life. Many also hoped to influence the celestial gods and thereby gain control of earthly happenings through magic and prayer. The second century Chaldean Oracles, admired by the later Neoplatonists, and the Greek 'Hermetic' writings produced in Egypt, were popular influences in which oracular prediction and magic were combined. Like the Gnostic literature, they were influenced by the philosophy of Plato, and especially by his view of the human soul as an exile from the celestial world, imprisoned in a corrupting body but able through purification to re-ascend to its original home.

Christianity, destined to be officially adopted and promoted by Constantine and to prevail over its rivals, offered spiritual fulfilment through prayer and sacraments, the hope of immortality, moral purpose, and membership of a supportive and socially caring community; and it also combined a universality of appeal, in the doctrine that all may be saved through grace, with an intellectually sophisticated theology. The claim that a particular people in history were chosen to reveal God's purpose, and that Christ was both God and Man, presented a challenge to reason which the early Fathers sought to meet with the aid of Greek, and especially Platonic, philosophy.

At Alexandria, the successive heads of the Christian School, Clement and Origen - the latter a contemporary of the young Plotinus and fellow student of his teacher Ammonius - taught that the best in Greek philosophy was a divine gift to lead men to

Christ, and that philosophy, while not necessary to salvation, was a valuable preparation for theology and aid to the reasoned explanation and defence of faith. Mankind universally, by their possession of reason, partake in the divine Logos - Reason or Word - which is manifested in Christ, who mediates between the transcendent deity and this world. The doctrine of Logos, both divine and immanent in the world, is a characteristic synthesis of scriptural and Greek thought, and the Platonic concepts of God, of the soul, of the relation of intelligible to material existence, and the description of creation in the *Timaeus* are also selectively used in theological exposition.

This early Christian Platonism had been anticipated by the first-century Jewish Alexandrian, Philo, who used Greek philosophy to support an allegorical interpretation of the Old Testament. There are close resemblances between the thought of Philo and Plotinus: God is the One, immutable, infinite and self-sufficient, and the Ideas are His thoughts; His first-born son, the Logos, Word or Wisdom, is the pattern and mediator of creation, the principle of order in the universe, and archetype of human reason; the goal of human life is the vision of God, to be achieved by ascetic liberation from body and the world.

Ascetic withdrawal from the world, and mortification of the flesh - sometimes taken to grotesque extremes - were a common religious response to the ills and fears of the third century. Egypt in this period saw the birth and rapid growth of Christian monasticism, originally a solitary life of prayer and contemplation. The community of 'Platonopolis' which Plotinus had hoped to found was no doubt intended in the same spirit for monastic retirement, not as a model Republic.

PLOTINUS IN HIS TIME

Although apparently indifferent towards religious cults, Plotinus is prepared to treat myth and ritual as repositories of ancient wisdom, susceptible to allegorical interpretation. The drama of myth reflects spiritual truths, dividing the indivisible and setting it in space and time, as metaphysical argument is also forced to do. The initiation ceremonies and secret revelations of the mysteries symbolise the inner purification, leading to mystical vision, in the life of the sage. Plotinus believed in the efficacy of prayer and magic and the possibility of astrological prediction, but there is no compelling evidence that he engaged in such practices himself. His interest in them is rather as signs of the spiritual harmony and interdependence of the universe. From time to time in the *Enneads* Plotinus recognises that reasoned demonstration is not always enough to convince the reader, and refers to the evidence of the senses and everyday experience, including religious practices, to strengthen conviction – *pistis* in Greek, the term for 'faith' in late Neoplatonist, and Christian, literature. To Christianity there are no explicit references in the *Enneads*, though there were Christians among the Gnostics who are the targets of the polemic in *Ennead* II 9. Gnostic doctrines were seen as a special threat by Plotinus, as they had invaded his own circle, and superficially might seem to resemble his own teaching.

Platonism in the third century was a flourishing tradition, and beginning to acquire a new significance in its application to Christian theology. Plotinus was important not in rediscovering a lost heritage, but in the particular emphases of his interpretation. Bearing in mind that the whole hierarchy of spiritual reality exists within the individual human soul, we may see the greater part of Plotinus' work as the exploration of the self in its complexity, the causes of its alienation and disharmony, and the means of its redemption. Descriptions of mystical union, though memorable, constitute only a very small part of his writings, but his dominant theme is the need to detach the soul from the body and external existence, and turn inwards.

By contrast with the disorder and misery of contemporary society, Plotinus represents reality as harmonious and ordered, everywhere tending towards the good under the direction of a rational Providence. The individual soul, discovering its identity with the All, has perfection within its reach, attainable by its own efforts. Evil and suffering cannot touch the true self, and external events and physical circumstances are irrelevant to happiness. Meaning and purpose in life are to be found in escape from the world, the withdrawal of the mind into itself; the sage is above the chances of this world. We know from Porphyry the name of one member of the senate at Rome, Rogatianus, who renounced his worldly goods under Plotinus' influence, and that the philosopher had a sufficient following to consider founding a new community. To his senatorial and educated audience, Plotinus offered consolation and a new purpose in place of the prevailing sense of helplessness, by an inversion of customary standards of what is real and important.

> When mortal men bear arms against each other, in ordered ranks, just as they do in sport in their war-dances, they demonstrate that all human concerns are but play, that deaths are of no account, and that to die in warfare and in battles is merely to forestall the fate of old age, departing sooner and returning sooner. If they are robbed of their wealth in their lifetime, they may reflect that it was not always theirs, and that the plunderer, robbed in his turn, is mocked by his possession; and that, in any case, to possess wealth is a greater evil than to

> lose it. Murders and all deaths, the sacking and plunder of cities should be observed as no more than a stage-play, with its changes of scene and costume and simulations of grief and lamentation. In the fortunes of this earthly life it is not the soul within, but the outer shadow of a man that weeps and laments and acts out its part; all the world is their stage, and they set up their stage in many parts of it. Such conduct belongs to a man who knows only the lower, external life, unaware that even his sincerest tears are but play. To engage seriously in matters of real moment is a life for the sage in man; the other man is a toy. (*Ennead* III 2.15)

If a sense of awe in the face of a higher reality and a striving for self-transcendence are criteria of religion, then the followers of Plotinus were invited to share a religious commitment along with philosophical dialectic. But it was religion of a cerebral kind, without rites, communal worship or prayer, without historical drama, and with an emotional appeal of limited scope.

Plotinus has sometimes been regarded as a mystagogue and obscurantist, who broke with the rationalist tradition of Greek philosophy. Such a view does not do justice to the range of issues raised or the quality of argumentation in the *Enneads*, nor to the supple and allusive style, and choice of imagery, by which he attempts to rouse in the reader a sense of the urgency of inexpressible experience. Modern scholars of Neoplatonism have made a much more positive assessment:

> Plotinus appears not as the subverter of the great tradition of Greek rationalism, but as its last constructive exponent in an anti-rational age ... what makes him exceptional in the third century is ... his resolute championship of reason as the instrument of philosophy and the key to the structure of the real. (Dodds, 1928, p.142)

The extracts from the *Enneads* which follow relate to the metaphysical system of Plotinus, his account of the human condition, and the path of ascent to spiritual perfection.

I

The One or Good

Summary

i) The variety of particular goods points to a supreme and self-sufficient Good, defined in Aristotle's phrase as 'that to which all things aspire', which transcends all other existence. The image of the Sun recalls the Myth of the Cave in Plato's *Republic* (Book VI), and the cult of the Sun was popular in the third century.

ii) The existence of an absolute, transcendental One is inferred from the necessity of unity in everything that exists. There are degrees of unity or participation in the One, the primal Unity.

iii) As Principle of all Being, and therefore 'beyond Being', the One must be infinite and without attributes; strictly, it transcends existence, knowledge and description. This 'negative theology' is derived from Plato's *Parmenides*.

In this and the following three extracts, the emphasis is on the inadequacy of human thought and language to express the transcendent Principle.

iv) The term 'One' is no more than an indicator of self-sufficient and infinite power (*dynamis*); neither Number nor Mind, God nor Good is an adequate title for him. In this extract the masculine pronoun is used; 'the One' and 'the Good' are neuter in Greek, but Plotinus uses both genders of the pronoun, even in a single sentence.

v) Images of the spring and the rooted tree: the Source is not spent in its creation.

vi) The necessity of 'negative theology': positive statements about the One are strictly inadmissible. Yet some knowledge of him is possible, both by inference from creation, and by a barely conscious awareness experienced during intellectual contemplation. Elsewhere, Plotinus describes the state of the mind in contemplation of the Intelligible in excited language, which contrasts with the still simplicity attained in ultimate union with the One. The comparison here with a poet or prophet in the grip of divine possession is striking.

vii) No duality, whether of subject and predicate or subject and object, can be admitted into the One. Plotinus therefore seeks to refute the Aristotelian doctrine of a self-thinking God – but only to propose as substitute a unique and immediate self-apprehension.

viii) Plotinus has argued that man is truly free only when willing and pursuing the Good, at the level of intellect. Here, he argues that the Good itself is free in a unique sense, by the identity of its will and existence. The extract is noteworthy for its insistence on the analogical nature of metaphysical language, and the need to negate one's terms, and then negate the negation, as the best approach to understanding the transcendent. Yet here also, more than anywhere, Plotinus characterises the One in boldly positive terms – Will, Love and Beauty.

ix) The eternal and spontaneous procession of the second and third hypostases from the One, and the creative power of contemplation in Intellect and Soul. The passage emphasises the continuity of the creative process, extending uninterrupted to the lowest forms of physical existence: the transcendent One is also immanent in every level of creation.

x) A highly positive description of the One as the cause of the eternal Beauty of the Intelligible. The One itself is Beauty only in a unique sense.

i) There must be one Good towards which all things tend

I 7.i

For anything that exists, how shall we define its good? It must surely be the natural activity of its life, and for any complex entity, will not its good be the proper, natural and never-failing activity of its better part? The soul's activity, therefore, will be its natural good; and if, as of the best nature itself, it directs its activity towards the highest good, this will be not merely the good in relation to the soul, but the Good absolutely. Then if there is a supremely good being, transcending all beings, which does not direct its activity towards another, but all others towards it, evidently this will be the Good by which all other things are enabled to participate in the good; and they that attain to the good in this way will do so both by becoming like the Good and by directing their activity towards it. If good, then, is activity which has the highest good as its aim, it follows that the Good itself does not look towards another or aspire to another, but is the still 'source and principle'[1] of natural activities, and creates all other things in the form of the good, and that not by directing its activity towards them, but as the goal to which they tend; and it is not by virtue of activity or thought that it is the Good, but by its very remaining in itself. Because it is 'beyond being',[2] it is beyond activity and beyond Mind and thought. And again, it must be supposed that the Good is that on which all things depend, while it depends on nothing; for only so is it true that the Good is 'that to which all things aspire'.[3] It must be, then, that the Good remains at rest, while all things turn towards it, as a circle turns towards the centre from which all its radii are drawn. We might compare it also to the sun, which is like a centre in relation to its own light, that depends on it and is everywhere linked to it and not severed; so that, even if you wish to part them, the light always stays with the sun.

ii) All particular existents depend upon the One
VI 9.i

All beings owe their being to the One, both the primary beings and those that in any degree are included among beings. For what could exist without being a unity? If things are deprived of the unity which is ascribed to them, they lose their identity. For example, an army does not exist unless it is one, nor do a chorus or a flock unless they are one. Further, there cannot be a house or a ship without unity, since the house and the ship are one, and were they to lose their unity, the house would no longer be a house nor the ship a ship. Continuous magnitudes, then, without the presence of unity, would not exist; at least, when divided, they change their being in proportion as they lose their unity.

Similarly with the bodies of plants and animals: each is a unity, and if they escape their unity, broken into fragments, they lose their former essence; no longer what they were but become new beings, these also dependent on their unity. Health, too, exists when the body is an ordered unity, and beauty when the principle of unity integrates the parts; and there is virtue in the soul when it is a unified whole in unitary concord. Since the soul, then, brings all things into one by fashioning, moulding, shaping and ordering them, ought we to say, now that we have come to it, that it is this that gives unity and this that is the One? No, but just as soul is not identical with the other gifts that it bestows on bodies, such as shape and form, which are distinct from it, so we must suppose that it gives unity, if it does give it, as something distinct from itself; and it is by looking towards the One that it makes each particular unity – making man, for example, in the image of Man, and including with the human form the unity within it. For each of what are called unities is one to the extent implied by its identity, so that lesser beings possess a lower degree, and greater beings a greater degree, of unity. The soul also, although distinct from the One, possesses a greater degree of unity in proportion to the greater reality of its being. Nonetheless, it is not the One itself, as the soul is a unity and its unity in a sense is accidental to it, and soul and unity are two, just as body and unity are two. Whatever is discontinuous, like a chorus, is at the furthest limit of unity, while what is continuous is closer; and soul, itself a participant in the One, is closer still. As to the proposal to identify soul and the One, because without unity soul would not even exist, we reply: first, that all other particular beings combine unity with their existence, yet they and the one are distinct – the body, for example, is not identical with unity, but partakes of unity; and second, that even the unitary soul, though not composed of parts, is multiple, since there are many powers in it, of reason, desire, perception, held together in unity as by a bond. The soul, therefore, being one itself, brings unity to another, and by another it is itself unified.

iii) The One is beyond description, except to point the way
VI 9.iii

The nature of the One, as the begetter of all things, is none of them. It is therefore not a determinate being, is without quality and quantity, and is neither intellect nor soul; it is not in motion nor yet at rest; not in place, not in time, but 'self-contained, unique in form'[4] – or rather, formless, existing before all form, before movement, before rest; for these are attributes of Being, which make it manifold. Why, then, if not in motion, is it not at rest? Because it is to Being that one or both of these must pertain, and Being is at rest in virtue of rest, and is not identical with rest; so it will have rest as an attribute and cease to be simple. Even to describe the One as cause is not to attach a predicate to the One, but to ourselves, because we take its gifts while it exists in itself. Strictly speaking, we should not say 'it' or 'exists', but we chase round about it in our desire to make sense of our experiences, at times coming close, but sometimes falling aside in the perplexity that it causes us.

VI 9.iv

The chief source of our perplexity is that awareness of the One comes not by knowledge or thought, as with all other intelligible realities, but by a presence superior to knowledge. The soul, in acquiring knowledge, abandons its full unity; for knowledge derives from reason, and reason entails plurality. The soul descends, therefore, into number and multiplicity, and deserts the One. We must progress beyond knowledge, therefore, and nowhere abandon unity, forsaking knowledge and its objects and every other vision, however beautiful. All beauty is consequent upon the One and issues from the One, as all the light of day comes from the sun. This is why Plato calls it 'not to be spoken or written';[5] yet we do speak and write of it, to guide men towards it and wake them from their reasoning to the vision, as if pointing the path to those who would contemplate. Teaching can show the way and the journey, but the vision of the One is then a task for those resolved to see it.

iv) The term 'One' implies infinite power and self-sufficiency

VI 9.vi

What meaning, then, do we give to the term 'One', and how should we accommodate it to our thought? We take it to be 'One' in a larger sense than that in which numerical unity or a point are one. For in mathematics the soul abstracts extension and plurality so as to arrive at the smallest possible term, and is focused on something indivisible in itself, but which was part of a divisible whole and belongs to another; whereas the One neither belongs to another nor is it part of what is divisible, and its indivisibility is not that of the smallest possible term. It is the greatest of all things, not in magnitude but in power, so that its power is in its absence of magnitude, just as its immediate sequels are indivisible and without parts in their powers, not in extension. He must also be taken to be infinite, not in the sense that his size or number are incalculable, but in that his power is beyond comprehension. For if you conceive of him as mind or god, he is more, and if you think of him as one, he is one in a larger sense than your thought could imagine; for he exists by himself, without attributes.

We might consider that his unity consists in his self-sufficiency; for as the most complete and self-sufficient of all things, he must also be the most without needs. Any manifold is deficient in its want of unity; for its parts are not unified and its being needs to be one. But the One does not need itself; for it is Unity itself. Certainly, any manifold needs all its members, and each component part is not independent but in need of its associates; there is deficiency, therefore, both in each several part and in the whole. If, then, there must be something completely self-sufficient, it must be the One, as it alone has no deficiency whether intrinsic or relative to another. It need seek nothing for its being, or its flourishing, or its transcendent status. The cause of all others, it owes its being to no other; and what outside itself could enhance its well-being? Nor is it by accident that it flourishes, as it is itself the Good. And it has no spatial location; for it needs no support, as if unable to bear itself up, and what needs support is lifeless body that falls if unsupported. All other things are established through him, who gave them their existence along with the place assigned to them; but to need a place is deficiency.

A principle has no need of its consequents, and the principle of all things has need of nothing. For whatever is deficient, is deficient in its search for its principle, and if the One is deficient it must be seeking not to be one; so it will be in need of its destroyer – but anything described as deficient is in need of the good that will preserve it. For the One, therefore, there is nothing that is its good, and so it wishes for nothing; it is beyond good and is itself the Good, not for itself but for all others that can participate in it. It does not think, or there would be diversity within it; nor does it move, being prior to movement and thought. For what will he think? Himself? In that case, before thinking he will be ignorant, and he, the self-sufficient, will need thought to know himself. Since, then, he neither knows nor thinks himself, there will be no ignorance in him; for ignorance implies a distinction of subject and object, but the Solitary neither knows nor has anything of which to be ignorant. It is One in union with itself, and has no need to think itself.

Indeed, to preserve its unity, we should not even attribute to it 'union with itself', but abstract from it thinking and union and thought of itself and everything else; we should rank it not with the thinker, but rather with thinking. Thinking does not think, but is the cause of thought in another; and the cause is not identical with the caused. The cause of all things is none of these things. So we should not even call it good after the good that it gives, but the Good in another sense, beyond all other goods.

v) The One is inexhaustible
III 8.x

What, then, is it? The power which generates all existence, without which the sum of things would not exist, nor would Intellect be the first and universal Life. What transcends Life is the cause of Life; for that activity of Life which is the sum of things, is not primal, but itself pours forth as if from a spring. Think of a spring, that has no further source, which gives itself entirely to rivers, yet is not exhausted by the rivers, but remains in its stillness; while the rivers issuing from it, before following their several courses, are undivided for a while, each knowing already where it will discharge its stream. Or think of the life which permeates a great tree while its source remains, not dispersed over the whole, but firmly grounded in the root, giving the plant all its manifold life yet remaining by itself, not manifold but the source of the manifold. And this is no wonder. Or rather, it is a wonder how Life in its multiplicity came from what is not multiple; and the multiplicity would not have existed unless before multiplicity there had been a simple Principle. The source is not fragmented into the universe; for its fragmentation would destroy the whole, which could no longer come to be if there did not remain by itself, distinct from it, its source. Universally, therefore, things go back to a Unity.

vi) Our knowledge of the One

V 3.xiv

How do we speak of the One? We certainly speak about it, yet it eludes our words and we have no knowledge or intuition of it. So how can we speak of it when it escapes our grasp? If knowledge cannot comprehend it, is it utterly beyond our reach?

We possess it, not so as to state it, but so as to speak of it allusively. We state what it is not, not what it is, and make inference to it from its sequels.

Yet though unable to state it, we are not debarred from possessing it. Those possessed and inspired by gods are at least aware that they hold within them something greater, though they know not what, and from their own movements and speech derive a kind of perception of what stirs them, a power not themselves. And this, it seems, is our relation to the One, when we function as pure intellect. We can divine that he is the inner Intellect, the giver of Being and all else of that order, but is himself none of these, something nobler than what is termed 'Being', greater than words can tell; for he surpasses speech, thought and perception, the author of all these but himself transcending them.

vii) The One, admitting no duality, does not even think himself
VI 7.xxxvii

Those who argue that thinking should be attributed to the Good do not suppose him to think of the lower forms of existence that derive from him - although others maintain that it is absurd that he should not have knowledge of everything. However, as they find nothing else more honourable than the Good, they attribute to him thought of himself, supposing that thought will enhance his dignity and that thinking is superior to his own essential nature, rather than that it is he who confers dignity on thought.

From what does his honour derive, from thinking or from himself? If from thinking, then by himself he is without honour, or less honourable; but if from himself, his perfection is prior to thinking and not completed by thinking. If it is because he is actuality, not potentiality, that he is supposed to think, and they maintain that his actuality is that of a being always in thought, they nevertheless give him two attributes, being and thought, in denial of his simplicity; for thought is an additional attribute to him, like actually seeing to the eyes even if they are always looking. And if they say that his actuality is the activity of thinking, yet thinking could no more think than movement could move.

'What? Do not you yourselves refer to those higher realities as Being and actuality?' So we do, but these are many and therefore differentiated, whereas the First is single, and it is to what is derivative that we attribute thought, and the search for its own being and self and for its Creator; and when it turns to this in contemplation and recognition, then it is properly called Intellect. But the First has not come to be and has nothing prior to it, but is always what it is; so what cause will it have to think? Plato is right, therefore, to say that it is above Intellect. If Intellect did not think, that would be a failure of Intellect; its very nature is to think, and if it were not to do so it would be unthinking. But why should we attribute a function to what has no function, and call it failure for not performing? One might as well call him unmedical. He has no function, because there is none allotted to him to perform. He is sufficient in himself, and needs to seek nothing beyond himself, transcending all that exists; for in being what he is, he is sufficient for himself and all existence.

VI 7.xxxviii

Yet even the word 'is' has no application to him, nor are the words 'he is good' appropriate, as they apply to what 'is'. The word 'is' is not used of him predicatively, but as identifying him. And when we talk of him as 'good', this is not to refer to him and predicate 'good' of him as an attribute, but to say that he and it are identical. But then, although we regard 'is good' and 'the Good' as inappropriate language, we cannot make ourselves clear if the word 'the' is eliminated entirely and so to avoid multiplying our terms we speak of 'the Good', so as to dispense with the 'is'.

But who will admit a nature that has not perception and knowledge of itself? What will he know, then? 'I am'? No, for he 'is' not. Why then shall he not say 'I am the Good'? Because again he will be predicating 'is' of himself. But suppose he says 'Good' only, with some addition; for one could think 'Good' without 'is' if one were not predicating it of something else. Yet he who thinks himself to be Good will inevitably think 'I am the Good'; otherwise, he will think 'Good' without entertaining the thought that he himself is this 'Good'. The thought, therefore, must be 'I am the Good'. And if the thought itself is the Good, it will not be thought of himself but of Good, and it will be thought, not himself, that is the Good. But if the thought of the Good is different from the Good, the Good is already there prior to the thought of it. And if the Good is sufficient in itself, prior to thought, then in being self-sufficient with respect to good it will have no need to think of itself. Therefore, it does not think itself as Good.

VI 7.xxxix

As what, then? There is nothing else that it thinks, it has only a simple apprehension of itself. But as there is no extension or diversity within it, what could that apprehension of itself be but itself?

viii) The One is uniquely free, an identity of Will and Being
VI 8.vii

A bold argument might be advanced against us, that the nature of the Good, as it merely happens to be what it is and is not master of what it is, is not the source of its own being, and will therefore have neither freedom nor the power of choosing whether to act or not, but will be subject to compulsion. This is a stubborn and difficult argument, which would entirely destroy the nature of voluntariness and self-determination and the concept of free-will, and render these ways of speaking idle, mere names with no basis in reality. For one who argues so must maintain not only that free-will does not exist, but also that he does not even understand the meaning of this word. If he agreed that he understands it, then he could easily be refuted, since the concept of free-will has application where he denied it. The concept is not concerned with being, nor is it applied to this – for it is impossible for anything to create itself and bring itself into existence; but rather, the idea seeks to distinguish, among existents, what is the slave of others, and what has self-determination, not subject to another but master of its own activity. This is clearly the case with eternal beings, inasmuch as they are eternal, and with those which pursue or possess the Good without hindrance. Of course, as the Good is above them all, to seek some other good beside it would be absurd.

Similarly, it is wrong to say that it exists by chance; for chance is found in multiplicity, at the later stages of creation, and we could not say that the First exists by chance and is not master of its own genesis – for he had no genesis. It is absurd to object that it acts in conformity with what it is, as if to claim that freedom only exists when there is action or activity contrary to nature. Nor, of course, is it deprived of free-will by being unique, if its uniqueness arises not from external constraint but from its very identity and self-contentment, and from having no superior; otherwise, one will be denying self-determination to what attains most completely to the Good. And if this is absurd, even more absurd would it be to deprive the Good itself of self-determination, because it is Good and remains by itself, not needing to move towards another, though all others move towards it, and with no need of anything. The truth is, that when its 'existence' and 'activity' are identical – for even in the realm of Intellect these are not to be distinguished, and action no more conforms to essence than essence to action – then the Good cannot act in conformity with its nature, nor will its activity and 'life' be referred to its essence, but its 'essence' is united and eternally co-existent with its activity; and the Good creates itself from both for itself, and belongs to nothing.

VI 8.ix

But if someone applied to the Good the word 'happened', we should not stop at the word but understand what the man who uses it means. What, then, does he mean? He means that it is the Principle by virtue of this particular nature and power that it possesses; for even if its nature were different it would be Principle with the nature that it possessed, and if it were inferior it would have acted in conformity with its own essence. To this we must reply that, as universal Principle, it was not possible for it to be what chanced, and not only could it not have an inferior nature, but it could not even be good in a different and defective sense of good. The Principle is necessarily superior to what is derived from it; it must therefore be something determinate. I mean determined by its uniqueness, not by constraint; for there was no constraint. Constraint belongs among beings derived from the Principle, and even this has no tyranny over them; but this uniqueness of the Good originates in the Good itself.

It is this, then, and not another, but what it must be; it did not, therefore, happen to be so, but was so of necessity; but this 'necessity' is a principle transcending all necessities. It will not then be a thing of chance; for it is not what chanced, but what must be; or rather, not even what must be – all creation must wait in suspense to see how the King will appear to them, and affirm his true nature, revealed not as a thing of chance but as true King, true Principle and true Good, not acting in conformity with the Good – or else he would seem to subserve another; rather, he is his one self, not acting in conformity with that One, but being that One.

But might it be objected that the One is thus, and only thus, and not otherwise? No, even the word 'thus' is inappropriate; for in using it you would be defining the One, and it would be something in particular. He who beholds it cannot say that it is 'thus', nor again 'not thus', for this would be to include it among the beings to which 'thus' is applicable. It is therefore beyond all beings which can be said to be 'thus'. Seeing it to be indefinable, you will deny to it all the descriptions applicable to its consequents; but if you must speak of it, you will describe it as omnipotence which is truly lord of itself, being what it wills to be; or rather, say that it has cast away 'what it wills' to the realm of Being, and is itself greater than all willing, setting will beneath it. It has not itself, then, willed its own 'thus', so as to conform to it, nor has another made it thus.

VI 8.xiii

Everything that exists, as long as it does not possess the Good, wills something beyond itself, but to the extent that it possesses the Good it wills itself, and such a presence is not by chance, nor is its essence apart from its will; and it is by this Good that each thing is defined and that it owns itself. If then it is by the Good that each thing creates itself, it surely becomes clear now that the Good, by which all other things are enabled to create themselves, will be what pre-eminently creates itself as it is, and that the will to be 'as it is' is united with its 'essence'. It is not possible to conceive of the Good without his willing to make himself what he is: his willing to be himself and his being what he wills run together; his will and self are one, and no less one for the objection that what he would have wished to be may be different from what he happened to be. For what could he have willed to be, except what he is? Even if we supposed that he could choose what he wished to become, and that it were possible for him to change his nature for another, he would not wish to become something else, nor would he censure himself as if constrained to be what he is – this 'being himself' which he has always willed, and wills. In reality, the nature of the Good is the willing of himself, not in the sense of a depraved subservience to his own nature, but in the sense that he chose himself since there was nothing else to beckon him. It might also be argued that nothing else includes in its essence the principle of self-contentment; even dissatisfaction with self is possible. But in the existence of the Good it must be that the choice and willing of itself are comprehended, or nothing could be self-contented; for other things are self-contented to the extent that they share in or imagine the Good. In speaking of the Good, we are forced to use words, by way of explanation, which should not strictly be applied to it, and should be allowed on the understanding that each is to be qualified by 'as it were'.

If, then, the Good exists, and choice and will together establish its existence – for without these it will not be; and if this Good must not be multiple: then its will and essence must be identified. But if its will is from itself, then its being also must be from itself, and our argument has discovered that he is his own creator. For if his will is from himself, and is, as it were, his function, and if this will is identical with his essence, then in this way he will be self-caused. He is therefore not what he chanced to be, but what he himself willed.

VI 8.xv

He is both object of love and love, and love of himself, in that he has beauty only from himself and in himself. He is in union with himself in the sense that same is united with same in a simple Unity.

ix) All things proceed from the One
V 2.i

The One is all things and yet no one of them. It is the source of all things, not itself all things, but their transcendent Principle; for in a way they move within the One – or rather, though not yet there, that is their destiny. How, then, do they derive from a single One, with no diversity apparent in it, no duality whatsoever? It is surely just because there is nothing in the One that all things proceed from it, and so that Being may exist the One is not Being, but the begetter of Being. This is the first act of generation: the One, perfect in seeking nothing, possessing nothing and needing nothing, overflows and creates a new reality by its superabundance; and its offspring turns to the One and is filled, and in contemplating the One becomes Intellect. Its stance towards the One gives it Being, while its contemplation of the One makes it Intellect; so in standing towards its source in contemplation it becomes at once Intellect and Being.

And being akin to the One, Intellect repeats the creative act, pouring forth power in abundance, in its own likeness, as its own prior poured forth power; and thus, from the essence of Intellect which remains unchanged, there issues the active power of Soul, as also Intellect issued from an unchanging One. But Soul is not changeless when it creates, but begets its image in movement; it becomes filled by contemplation of its source, but begets its image by a contrary, downward movement, and this image is sensation and the growth principle in plants.

Nothing is detached or severed from its prior, so that the higher soul seems to extend as far as plants; and in a way it does so extend, because the life in plants belongs to it. Not that soul is wholly within plants, but only to the extent that they are the lower limit of its advance, another level of existence created by its decline towards the worse. Its higher part is attached to Intellect, and allows Intellect to remain undisturbed.

x) The One, without form, is the transcendent source of all beauty
VI 7.xxxii

Where then is he who made this great beauty and this splendid Life, the begetter of Being? You see the beauty that plays upon all the forms themselves in their intricate variety. It is beautiful to linger in contemplation of this, yet in the midst of beauty you should look to see their source, and the source of their beauty. This cannot be any one of the forms, for then it would be only some part of them. It cannot, therefore, be a form or power of this kind, nor anything that has come to be and exists in the Intelligible, but must transcend all powers and all forms. The Principle is the formless, not in the sense of needing form, but as the origin of every form possessed of Intellect. The reality that proceeds from it necessarily assumes some determinate identity and takes its own particular form; but who could create something of what no one created? This, then, is none of the beings that are real, yet is all of them: none of them, because they are subsequent to it, but all of them, because they derive from it. What magnitude could he have, who has power to create all things? He would surely be infinite, but if infinite, then without magnitude. There is magnitude at the very extremity of creation, and its creator must have no magnitude himself. Besides, the greatness of real Being is not quantitative, but something else might have magnitude, dependent upon him. His own greatness is that nothing has more power than he and nothing may be compared to him; for under what aspect should he be equalled, being unique? He is eternal and extends through all creation, yet is without measure - but not measureless; or how might he be the measure of all things? Nor again, therefore, does he have form. In truth, an object of desire without form and shape to grasp will be of all things most desirable and lovable, and the love for it will be immeasurable. Love here has no limit, because the beloved has no limit, and love of him would be unbounded. So his beauty also is of another kind, Beauty that transcends beauty. For how could it have beauty, which has no being? But it is lovable and will beget beauty. So it is the power that begets all that is beautiful, and the bloom upon it, Beauty that creates beauty. And it not only begets beauty but makes it yet more beautiful by the Beauty that overflows from itself, as the source of beauty and the limit of beauty.

REFERENCES

1. Plato, *Phaedrus*, 245 c9.
2. Plato, *Republic*, 509 b9.
3. Aristotle, *Nichomachean Ethics*, 1094 a3.
4. Plato, *Symposium*, 211 b1.
5. Plato, *Letter VII*, 341 c5.

II
Intellect

Summary

i) True Being is distinguished from material existence, which derives from it at a lower level of creation, and its essential properties are stated. The triad Being-Life-Intellect was used by the later Neoplatonists to define the three aspects of Being – in itself, in its outgoing and in its inward return. Plato, in a unique passage (*Sophist* 248e) attributes motion, life, soul and wisdom to Being.

ii) Physical analogies and human relationships are used to bring out essential features of creative emanation: it is continuous, and the higher level of reality is imparted to the lower without being diminished; at each level, the offspring is necessarily less perfect than its begetter, to which it has a natural longing to return. Both Intellect and Soul are called Logos of their prior hypostasis, that is, they represent it as formative and regulative principles at a lower level of creation.

The concluding words, 'only separated by otherness', mean that the Good, though transcendent, is also immanent in every part of its creation, and not spatially separate.

iii) The two 'moments' in the creation of Intellect: the unformed pre-Intellect, and the filling of Intellect with intelligible forms, the multiple image of the One.

iv) The knowledge possessed by Intellect is immediate intuition of self-evident truths. Neither 'Intellect' nor 'Mind', therefore – both used in this translation – is an ideal rendering of the Greek *Nous*, but alternatives such as 'Intelligence', 'Spirit' or 'Intuition' are at least as misleading.

It is argued that such knowledge entails the identity of Intellect with the Intelligible beings that it thinks.

Elsewhere, Plotinus likens Intellect to sense-perception to the extent that both involve direct acquaintance with their objects: 'sense-perceptions here are dim intellections, while intellections There are clear perceptions' (VI 7.vii).

The later Athenian School, for whom every conceptual distinction stood for a real, existent recognised a triad of intelligible, intelligible-intellectual and intellectual gods.

v) A vivid impression of the life of the Intelligible beings, in which, despite their eternal and changeless nature, there is emphasis on movement. By their complete interpenetration, each member contains all the others, but its specific identity is given by its dominant part - an idea that goes back to Anaxagoras.

The 'greatest kinds' of Plato's *Sophist* - Being, Motion, Rest, Sameness and Otherness - are portrayed here as activities identical with Intellect.

'The life of ease' is a Homeric phrase used of the gods of Olympus.

vi) The Intelligible world contains perfect archetypes of everything that exists in the world of sense, of which, through the mediation of Soul, it is the creator. It is of Intellect that the terms 'God' and 'the Divine' are most often used.

The concluding sensuous image is suggestive of the mystical state of mind to which intellectual contemplation may lead, prior to the final union with the One.

vii) The ideal forms contained in the Intelligible include not only generic forms like Man, but forms of individuals. This doctrine, clearly stated here, is not in Plato, and was disputed by other Platonists; it refers to the individual soul, and testifies to the unique value of the personal self in Plotinus' thought.

Certain other passages in the *Enneads* which deny the reality of forms of individuals refer to physical phenomena.

viii) The life of Being is Eternity, fullness of life in a limitless present. Man in his Intellect is an inhabitant of Eternity.

This conception of Eternity entered Christian theology.

ix) Even Intelligible beauty can be uninspiring unless illumined by the light of the Good. This extract is notable for its assertion that the Good implants in every soul a love of him which only he can satisfy, and for its rejection of a purely formal conception of Beauty.

The phrase from Plato's *Phaedrus* refers to the impact of Beauty on the soul; Plotinus borrows it to describe indifference to Beauty.

x) Two dynamic images show how Being is identically present in every part of creation.

i) The nature of Being
III 6.vi

Being, properly so called, means authentic Being, or, in other words, Being without qualification, that nowhere falls short of Being. Perfect in Being, it needs nothing to preserve it in Being, but is the cause of that semblance of Being possessed by all other seeming realities.

If this is correct, then Being must be in life, and in perfect Life; if it fails of this, it will be no more Being than non-Being. It must therefore be Intellect, and Wisdom in perfection, and so defined and bounded; and its power must be all-inclusive and without limit, if it is to have no defect. It must also be eternal, changeless, entirely unreceptive and impenetrable; for if receptive, it would embrace what is other than itself, or non-Being. It must be Being entire, and therefore possess of its own resource all that pertains to Being, all gathered together and all a unity.

If, then, we define Being in these terms - and we must, or Intellect and Life would not originate in Being, but be imported into Being from non-Being, and be unreal; and Being would be devoid of Life and Intellect, which would be attributes of what is really non-Being, the lower derivatives of Being: if, then, we recognise that only the One prior to Being has no need of Life and Intellect, though imparting them to Being, and we define Being in these terms, then Being cannot be corporeal or the substrate of material things, but their existence is the existence of the unreal.

ii) The generation of Intellect and Soul

V 1.vi

All existing things, as long as they survive, necessarily give out into the world a mode of existence that plays about them and derives from their present power, like an image of the archetypes which gave it birth. Fire, for example, gives out heat from itself, and cold surrounds the snow that also contains it. But the best testimony comes from sweet-scented objects, which as long as they exist diffuse an aura about themselves that makes the bystander delight in their being. Further, everything that attains to perfection begets offspring, and the One that is always perfect begets eternally, and its offspring is less than itself. What then must we say of the most perfect? That nothing derives from it but what is next to it in greatness. And next to it in greatness, and second, is Intellect; for Intellect beholds him and needs him alone, while he has no need of Intellect. The offspring of one higher than Intellect is Intellect, and Intellect is higher than all things, because all else is subsequent to it; Soul is a formative power and activity of Intellect, just as Intellect is of the One. In Soul, a phantom of Intellect, the formative power is faint, and it must therefore look towards Intellect; and Intellect similarly must look towards the One, in order to be Intellect. It sees him because it is not parted from him, but succeeds him with nothing between, as Soul, too, is not parted from Intellect. Everything longs for and loves its father, and especially when father and offspring are alone; but when the Father is the supreme Good, its offspring is with it of necessity, only separated by otherness.

iii) Two moments in the generation of Intellect

VI 7.xv

This Life, then, in its all-embracing variety and primal unity – who could see it without longing to share in it, disdaining all other life? For all lower life is darkness, trivial, faint and cheap, impure itself and defiling the pure; and if your gaze is set on this, you no longer see nor live those pure lives, all in a unity, in which there is nothing that does not live and live in purity, without taint of evil. Evils are here below, where only a trace of Life, a trace of Intellect, exist; but There is the archetype, '*in the form of Good*', as Plato says, because it possesses the Good in ideal forms.

The One is the Good, and Intellect is good by virtue of its life of contemplation; for the objects of its consciousness are in the form of Good, and it was by contemplation of the nature of the Good that it came to own them. They entered into it not as they were in the Transcendent, but taking form in the moment of their possession by Intellect. The Good is the Principle: from him the forms entered Intellect, and Intellect made them by its vision of the Good.

It was not ordained that Intellect, in its gaze towards the Good, should be unthinking, nor again that its thoughts should be in him, if Intellect was to give them birth. And so from the Good it derived the power of generation, of filling itself with its own offspring, the gift of the Good yet not contained in him. While he is One, the forms in Intellect are multiple, since Intellect, unable to sustain the power bestowed on it, broke it in pieces, that what it could not hold in unity it might bear divided.

All that it brought to birth came from the power of the Good, and in the form of Good; and Intellect is good, a complex good, because constituted by forms that reflect the Good. We might compare it to a living, variegated sphere, or imagine it as something full of faces, gleaming with living faces, or as pure souls, all running into one, nowhere deficient but in all their perfection; and all-embracing Intellect enthroned upon them, and the place illumined by the light of Intellect: but to imagine it so would be to see it as if from outside, as distinct from it; the task is to become it, and make ourself the vision.

VI 7.xvi

When Intellect looked towards the Good, did it think that One as multiple, and, while one itself, did it think him as many and divide him in itself, unable to hold him entire in its thought?

No, it was not yet Intellect when it looked towards the One, and no thought accompanied its gaze. We should rather say that as yet it did not even see the One, but lived towards it, dependent on it and turned to it, and this movement became filled, by moving There about the One, and made Intellect full, and was no longer merely movement, but movement sated and full; and it then became all things, and came to know this in its own self-awareness, and it was now Intellect, filled with forms for contemplation and beholding them by a light granted, like the forms, by the Good.

iv) Intelligible beings cannot be external to Intellect

V 5.i

Might it be held that Intellect, the true and authentic Intellect, will sometimes fall into error and believe falsehoods? By no means: for if it were unintelligent, how could it still be Intellect? It must be for ever in a state of knowledge, and never forgetful, and its knowledge must not be based on conjecture, or uncertain, or accepted on report. Nor, then, can it be derived from demonstration; for even if some knowledge by demonstration were attributed to it, it would still have knowledge of self-evident truths. In fact, reason suggests that all its knowledge is of this kind, since there will be no means of distinguishing between what is self-evident and what is not. But be that as it may; let us ask, where self-evidence is admitted, how it can be that such knowledge presents itself to Intellect with immediate certainty. Whence comes the conviction of its truth?

Even that knowledge derived from sense-perception that seems most patently reliable is subject to doubt, in case the apparent reality of its objects belongs not to objective existents but to subjective states of the percipient, and needs intellect or reason to interpret it. Even when it is agreed that the objects of sense-perception, to be apprehended by the senses, are real, what is known by sense-perception is an image of the object; the senses cannot grasp the object itself, which remains beyond their reach.

Now, if the knowing Intellect is to encounter the intelligible realities that are the objects of its knowledge, how can they be distinct from it? For if they were, it might not encounter them; and so it would be possible for it not to know them, or only to know them on its encounters with them, with the consequence that its knowledge would not be perpetual. If Intellect and intelligibles are said to be conjoined, we shall ask what this conjoining means. Further, intellections, like sense-perceptions, will be images, and therefore impressions made by external objects. But how are such impressions possible? What shape can they have? And intellection, like sense-perception, will be of what is external. Will it differ, then, except in apprehending less extended objects? How will it know that its knowledge is real? How will it recognise an instance of Goodness, Beauty or Justice? For each of these will be distinct from Intellect, and the principles of judgement by which it will be guided will not be internal to it, but lie outside it, as will Truth itself.

Again, intelligible forms are either senseless and devoid of life and intellect, or they possess intellect. If they possess intellect, then both the Intelligible and Intellect, and so Truth, are found here together, and this is the primal Intellect; and we shall enquire into the nature of the Truth here identified, as to whether the Intelligible and Intellect while conjoined in a single reality, remain a duality and distinct from each other, or some other relation holds. On the other hand, if intelligible forms are senseless and without life, what kind of realities are they? They are certainly not premises, axioms or predicates, since they would then not have real existence themselves, but only make statements about other realities – that 'Justice is beautiful', for example, where Justice and Beauty are distinct from the words.

If intelligible forms like Justice and Beauty are held to be simple and separate entities, then the Intelligible will not be a unity or in unity, but each form will be set apart from the others. Where will they be, and at what points in space will they be segregated? How will Intellect encounter them in its travels? How will they continue in being, or continue in the same place? Whatever shape or configuration will they possess? Perhaps they stand revealed like figures of gold or some other material made by a sculptor or engraver? But if so, the Intellect which contemplates them will be sense-perception. And why should one of these be the form of Justice, and another something else?

But the most serious difficulty of all is this. However ready one might be to allow that intelligibles are external, and that Intellect contemplates them as external, it must follow that it cannot possess the truth of them, and that it is deceived in everything it contemplates. For while they would be the authentic realities, it will contemplate them not as possessing them but as receiving images of them, and its knowledge of them will be no more than this. It will not, then, possess authentic reality, but will receive in itself images of the truth, and so possess falsities and no truth at all. If it knows that it possesses falsities, it will admit that it has no access to the truth; but if even this knowledge escapes it, and it mistakes what it possesses for the truth, then the double error will further distance it from truth.

This is the reason, I believe, why there is no truth, but only opinion, in sense-perceptions; it is opinion because it receives impressions, and the impressions that it receives and possesses are distinct from their source.

And so, if there is no truth in Intellect, then such an Intellect will not be truth, nor truly Intellect; and there will be no Intellect at all. Yet truth will not be found elsewhere.

V 5.ii

One must not, therefore, seek the Intelligible outside Intellect, or talk of Intellect receiving images of reality, for this is to exclude Intellect from truth, render the Intelligible unknowable and non-existent, and finally abolish Intellect itself. On the contrary, if knowledge and truth are to be admitted, and real Being protected, along with knowledge of the essence of each intelligible reality; and if we are to know not merely the qualities of a thing, those reflections and traces of reality, but possess those realities themselves, living and identified with them: then they must all be included within the authentic Intellect. Only so will it know them, and its knowledge be genuine; and it will never forget or wander in search of them; and the truth will be in it as the seat of all Being, which will be living, active Intellect. These riches must be of the essence of that divine Principle – or where will be its worth and its grandeur?

Again, only so is it dispensed from demonstration and persuasion; for it is itself the Truth, and self-evident. It knows its principle by its own derivation, and it knows derived existence to be itself – the Intelligible, the Real; it is its own surest witness. Real truth is a harmony not with another, but with itself; it affirms nothing beside itself, at once the reality that it affirms and self-affirmation.

V 8.vi

I believe that the wise men of Egypt, either by scientific knowledge or innate understanding, did not use alphabetic symbols which spell out words and sentences, and which imitate sounds and the utterance of propositions, but expressed their meaning more cleverly by drawing images; and in representing each single idea by a single image inscribed in their temples, they exhibited the non-discursive thought of Intellect. For each image is a kind of knowledge and wisdom, a self-evident reality, not a process of discursive and deliberate thought.

v) The life of the intelligible gods

V 8.iii

As to the nature of Intellect within the gods, we may learn it from the intellect within us, when purified - or, if you like, from the gods themselves. For indeed, all the gods are sublime and beautiful, and their 'beauty unimaginable';[1] but what makes them so? It is surely Intellect, and Intellect so intensely active in them as to be visible. It is not, of course, because of their corporeal beauty; for those who have bodies are not gods in virtue of this, but even these are gods in virtue of their intellect. They are beautiful by their godhead. They are not wise and foolish by turns, but for ever wise in the serene and changeless purity of Intellect, all-knowing, attentive not to human affairs but to their own divine realm, and all that falls within the view of Intellect. The gods in heaven, being at leisure, for ever contemplate, though as if from afar, the life of that still higher heaven to which they raise their heads; while the gods in that higher heaven, all those whose dwelling is upon it and within it, know all that heaven by their presence in every part of it.

For all things there are heaven, and earth and sea and animals and plants and mankind are heaven; everything is heavenly in that higher heaven; and the gods there, not disdaining mankind or anything else there, because they belong among those heavenly forms, traverse all that country and space at their ease.

V 8.iv

For it is 'the life of ease' there, and Truth is their mother, their nurse, their being, and their sustenance; and they see all things, those to which not genesis but real Being belongs, and themselves in the others. For all are transparent, nothing dark or opaque, each wholly revealed to each to its inmost part; for light is transparent to light. For each holds all things in himself, each sees all in every other, so that all things are everywhere, all is all and each is all, and the glory unbounded; for each of them is mighty, even the small is mighty, and the sun there is all stars, and each star the sun and all stars. In each a different form prevails, but all forms are found in it. Movement, also, is pure there, not confounded by alien mover; and rest is untroubled, undisturbed by the restless; and beauty is sheer beauty, because not set in the unbeautiful. Each walks not as on alien ground, but each one's place is its essential self, and in its ascent its station accompanies it; being and place are not distinct. Its ground is Intellect, its very self is Intellect; as one might imagine that in this visible and luminous heaven of ours the radiance that shines from it formed the substance of the stars. In this world the separate parts do not issue from each other, and each can be only a part; but in that higher world each form issues eternally from the whole, and is at once individual and the whole. It bears the semblance of a part, but the keen-sighted there can see the whole within it, just as they say that Lynceus observed the inner depths of the earth, in a myth that tells of the eyes of the intelligible gods. No weariness attends their contemplation there, and no satiety to give them pause; for there was never emptiness to fill, and bring to final satisfaction. Where none differs from another, there is no room for mutual resentments. And all are changeless there. They want full satisfaction only in not disdaining the source of their fulfilment: to see is to continue in the vision, to behold infinity in themselves and the objects of their contemplation, in obedience to their nature. No one whose life is pure finds life wearisome: how then should the best life hold weariness? Their life is wisdom, and wisdom not supplied by reasoning, because eternally complete and perfect, not needing investigation; this is the primal and underived Wisdom, and Wisdom not acquired by Intellect, but its very essence.

vi) The living world of Intellect comprises forms of everything in the world of sense

VI 7.xii

Since we maintain that this universe is like a model of that higher world, the living universe must have a prior existence there, and everything must be there if it is to be the totality of Being. The heaven there must be a living being, and therefore a heaven not bare of what here are called stars; for how could there be heaven without stars? Earth also surely exists there, not a barren earth, but one far more instinct with life, and all the living creatures are in it that walk on land in this world, and all plants surely rooted in life; and there is sea there, and all water in a living and unending stream, and all living creatures of the water; and air is an element of that universe, and there are living creatures of the air in it conformable to the air itself. The members of that living reality must surely be alive, as they are even in this world; and every living creature must exist there, of necessity. As are the great regions of the universe, so must be the living creatures that inhabit them. The heaven there, by the very mode of its being, determines the being and the form of all creatures that live within it, and their existence is necessary; if this were not so, there could be no heaven or earth or sea there.

To seek the origin, therefore, of these living creatures is to seek the origin of that heaven; and this is to seek the origin of living Being, which is to seek the origin of Life, and universal Life, and universal Soul and universal Mind. In truth, there is no penury or want there, but all things are teeming and seething with Life. All flow from one spring, not like a single current of breath or warmth, but as it were a single quality enclosing all qualities in its keeping; sweetness with fragrance, the taste of wine and the savours of every juice, all colours known to sight and textures known to touch, along with all sounds that meet the ear, all melodies and all rhythm.

vii) Ideal forms of individuals

V 7.i

Is there an ideal form of each individual? If I and each individual have a way of ascent to the Intelligible, then the principle of each of us is there. If Socrates, the soul of Socrates, always exists, there will be an ideal Form of Socrates.

But if he does not always exist, but the former Socrates becomes a different soul at different times - Pythagoras, for example, or someone else - then it will no longer be true that this particular individual exists also in the Intelligible.

However, if the soul of each individual contains the formative principles of everyone that it successively occupies, then again all will exist in the Intelligible; and we do say that each soul contains all the formative principles in the universe. If, therefore, the universe contains the principles not only of man but of each individual animal, then so does the soul; and the number of formative principles will then be infinite, unless the universe recurs in cycles, and infinity is thereby brought within limit by the re-birth of the same individuals.

Then if a single archetype is instantiated many times, what need is there of a principle and archetype for every existent within a single cycle? Surely one Man is sufficient for all men, just as a limited number of souls produce an unlimited number of men?

No, the same principle cannot account for different individuals, nor is Man a sufficient exemplar for the totality of particular men, distinct from each other not only in their material constituency, but also in countless formal characteristics. Men are not like portraits of Socrates in relation to the original; their different compositions must derive from different forming principles. The universal cycle contains all the principles of form, and when it recurs it re-produces the same existents in the image of the same principles. There is no need to fear that this account introduces infinity into the Intelligible; it is an infinity contained in indivisible unity, and it advances, as it were, in its periodic acts.

viii) The life of intelligible Being is Eternity

III 7.v

Whenever I encounter something with my mind such that I can say of it, or rather see, that its existence is wholly without beginning - for otherwise it would not be everlasting, or at least not everlasting in its entirety - is this sufficient ground for calling it eternal? Rather, its intrinsic nature should be such as to give confidence that it will remain as it is, unchanging, so as to be found the same under any future observation. Now suppose that, instead of withdrawing from the contemplation of it, one were to stay in its company, marvelling at its nature, and enabled to do so by an unfailing power within oneself. Surely this would be to enter eternity oneself, with all the fullness of one's being, to be assimilated to it and be made eternal, contemplating eternity and the eternal by the eternal in oneself. If this, then, is the condition of what is eternal and everlasting, to be in all respects unchanging, and to possess life in ever-present completeness, without past, present or future increment, then such a being will be eternal.

Eternity, therefore, is an awesome state, which the mind identifies with God, the God in the Intelligible. And eternity could be fairly described as God revealing and displaying his true nature, as Being undisturbed and changeless, ever determinate and well-grounded in its life. If we ascribe plurality to eternity, this is no wonder, since every intelligible being is multiple in its limitless power; to be limitless is to be never-failing, and eternity is this pre-eminently, because it never spends itself. And if one were to describe Eternity as Life in a limitless present, a wholeness of Being not dispersed into past or future, one would be close to defining it.

III 7.vi

Being so defined, so consummately beautiful and everlasting, is centred in the One, from which it issues and towards which it tends, never departing from it but remaining always around it and within it, and living by its law; and Plato, I believe, made a profound and pertinent judgement in these words, 'eternity remains in unity',[2] meaning that it not only draws itself into self-contained unity, but is the Life of unchanging Being encircling the One. This, then, is what we are seeking, and to remain thus is Eternity.

ix) Even the beauty of intelligible forms is dead unless enlivened by the light of the Good.

VI 7.xxi

Just as with material objects, infused though they are with light, there is yet need of another light, so that their own light, which is the colour in them, may be visible; so too the intelligible forms, though full of light, need another, greater light to reveal them to themselves and others.

VI 7.xxii

When we see this light, then indeed we are impelled towards them in longing, rejoicing at the light that plays over them, as with the objects of earth our love is not for their matter, but for the Beauty reflected in them. Each has its own identity, but becomes an object of desire when the Good colours it, lending it graces and prompting desire in its lovers. And so the soul, taking in that outpouring from the Divine, is stirred to frenzy and goaded to passion, and becomes love. Before this, even Intellect with all its beauty cannot move it; for that is a dead beauty, until lit by the Good, and the soul by itself 'falls back and lies supine',[3] wholly unmoved, and, in the presence of Intellect, indifferent. However, let there but enter into soul a glow of warmth from the Divine, and it will grow strong and awaken and truly spread wings; and though charmed by the proximate object it will be lifted in recollection to a greater reality. So long as a still higher summit remains, its nature is to rise again, lifted by the Giver of that love. And while it rises beyond Intellect, it cannot run beyond the

Good; for beyond that nothing lies. If soul remains in Intellect, it has a fair and noble vision, but falls short of all it seeks, as if it encountered a face which, though beautiful, still lacks the power to catch the eye, because no grace plays on its beauty to enhance it. In this world of sense, also, we must insist that Beauty is not symmetry but the light that illumines symmetry, and that it is this that inspires our love.

For why does the light of beauty shine more on a living face, and only a trace on the dead, though the flesh and proportions are not withered? Why are livelier statues more beautiful, though others be better proportioned? Why a living man, though uglier, more beautiful than a sculptured beauty? Surely, because what has life is more desirable; and this because it has soul; which is to say, it is more informed by the Good. Then it is coloured, in a sense, by the light of the Good; and the soul so illumined awakens and rises up, and lifts what it possesses, making it good to its capacity and waking it into life.

x) Being is identically present everywhere
VI 4.vii

Let us again ask how Being can be present identically in everything, which is equivalent to the question how each of the manifold and separate objects of sense partakes of the same Being. Our account refutes the conception of Being as fragmented among multiple participants, and shows rather that the manifold should be brought under the unity; that unity has not been dispersed into them, but they by their dispersal have made it seem divided – as if the principle of control and cohesion should be divided equally with its material.

And yet a hand might control an entire object such as a long piece of wood, and while the control of the hand extends over the whole, it is not divided part for part with the material it controls; the extent of its power, it seems, is proportionate to its grip, but the hand has its own magnitude, not that of the object that it lifts and controls. Add another length to the object and, if the hand can bear it, the power will control that also, without being divided proportionately among the lengths of wood. And now abstract the physical presence of the hand, but keep the same power by which the hand supported the object: would not the same power, undivided, be equally present in every part of the object?

Again: imagine a small luminous object placed at the centre of a larger, transparent sphere, so that the light from the inner object shone throughout the enclosing sphere, and this was its sole source of light; should we not say that the inner source has reached every part of the outer mass, while itself remaining unchanged, and that the light visible in the small object has occupied the other? Now it is not by being physically extended that the small object radiates light: it is not as body, but as luminous body that it possesses light, and by a different, incorporeal power. So abstract the extended object, but keep the power of the light: would you still locate the light in a particular spot, or would it be equally present throughout the whole outer sphere?

VI 4.viii

Since light, then, belongs to a material object, it is possible to specify its source by stating the position of the object. But an immaterial nature, prior to material existence and therefore independent of body, and self-grounded – or better, in need of no such ground: how could such a nature, without point of origin or spatial or material location, be described as divided, part here, part there? This would be to specify a place of origin and material location. It follows, therefore, that its every participant partakes of the power of Being in its entirety, while Being is unchanged and undivided.

REFERENCES

1. Plato, *Republic*, 509 a6.
2. Plato, *Timaeus*, 376 d6.
3. Plato, *Phaedrus*, 254 b8.

III
Soul

Summary

i) Against philosophers, such as Numenius, who posited more than one divine Intellect, Plotinus insists on the necessity of only three hypostases. Soul in its highest phase, whether World Soul or individual soul, transcends the physical and enjoys eternal contact with Intellect. The 'mediate soul' is the reasoning faculty; the 'law' (*themis*) is a religious term, and refers here to governing Providence.

ii) After refuting the accounts of soul taught by other schools of philosophy, including the materialism of the Stoics, the harmony theory of the Pythagoreans, and Aristotle's doctrine of *entelechy* (immanent form of a living body), Plotinus uses Platonic arguments to establish the immortality of the incorporeal soul, as the cause of life and movement.

iii) The unplanned and spontaneous creation of the material world by the lower Soul, or Nature, contrasts with pictures of creation as conscious design, such as are found in Plato's *Timaeus* and in Jewish and Christian literature. 'My Mother and the beings that begot me ... principles of higher ancestry' are the higher Soul and its formative principles (*logoi*).

At the end of the extract, the analogy with human affairs shows Plotinus' poor estimate of the life of action, as a kind of perversion of contemplation.

In Plotinus' universe all living creatures are contemplative, in the degree that their nature permits.

iv) The emergence of the material world, though a descent in the creative procession, is yet necessary for Soul to express itself; the darkness at the furthest limits is Matter.

Two memorable images are used to convey that Soul at once transcends the universe yet is everywhere present to it.

v) Plato in the *Timaeus* defined Time as a 'moving image of eternity' (37d5), and Plotinus here as 'the life of the Soul in movement'. Whereas the thought of Intellect is immediate intuition in a boundless present, the characteristic activity of Soul is the sequential process of discursive reason.

The 'restless nature' that separates from Intellect is Soul. This passage emphasises the negative aspects of Soul's emergence: self-assertion, and dissipation of creative power (the image of the seed).

vi) As often when trying to state spiritual realities, Plotinus has recourse to physical analogies in explaining that Soul is never parted, but everywhere omnipresent.

vii) In the ensoulment of particular bodies, under the direction of the World Soul, the individual soul instinctively fulfils the law of creation.

viii) On the other hand, its separation from its Principle may be interpreted as an act of self-will, a dishonouring of its higher nature by immersion in body.

Ennead V 1 is the treatise most often quoted by the Christian Fathers. The Plotinian self-assertion of souls, being a necessary part of creation, is not sin in the Christian sense.

ix) Individual souls are one with the World Soul, and to reflect on this will be the first step towards liberating the soul from body and restoring its relationship with divine Being.

The words 'hateful to the gods', applied here to matter, are used of Hades by Homer.

i) Soul's relation to the One and Intellect
II 9.ii

We must not, therefore, posit more than three hypostases, nor make superfluous distinctions between intelligible realities which their nature will not admit. We must insist that there is one Intellect, unchangeably the same, not subject to decline, and to the best of its powers an image of its Father; and that as to our Soul, one part is for ever in contact with the Intelligible, one part concerned with this world of sense, and a third part holds a mediate position. Soul is one nature in multiple powers, and sometimes is wholly borne along with its best part, that belongs to real Being, while at other times its basest part is drawn downwards, drawing the mediate soul with it, though the law forbids the whole soul to decline. Soul suffers this misfortune for not remaining in the realm of Beauty, the home of Soul intact and undivided, where we ourselves have no mere partial being; from where it gives of itself to the material world all that it can receive, itself remaining undisturbed, and ruling not by rational plan or interference, but imparting order with marvellous power by the contemplation of its higher origin. The more it stays rapt in that vision, the greater is its grace and power; and enriched by it, it gives to its creation, illumined always as it illumines.

ii) Soul, as the source of all that lives, must be life essentially, and so immortal

IV 7.viii

What degree of existence belongs to Soul? If it is neither material body nor affection of body, but action and creation, the spring and origin of manifold existence, it must be a substance of a different order from corporeal existence. It is clearly what we declare to be real Being. Everything corporeal may be described as Becoming, not Being, as what 'comes to be and perishes, but never really is',[1] as what is merely preserved by participation in Being, as far as it may.

IV 7.ix

The contrary nature, which has Being of itself, is all that Reality which knows neither birth nor destruction; for otherwise all existence would pass away, never to return, at the death of what sustains it; and even this whole Universe is preserved and set in order by the Soul. Soul is 'the principle of motion',[2] the self-moved cause of movement in the world, and source of life to ensouled body, while itself essentially life, and therefore life eternally. For not everything can have a borrowed life, or there would be an infinite regress: there must be a nature that has life in a primal sense, necessarily indestructible and immortal, because the source of life to all others. And this is where all that is divine and blessed must be set, the source of its own life and being, possessed of primal Being and primal Life, unchanging in its essence, knowing neither birth nor death.

From where could it come to be, or into what could it dissolve? If real Being must be attributed to it, its Being cannot come and go with time; no more can white, the colour, be now white but now not white. If white were real Being as well as white, it would be eternal; but whereas white is merely white, whatever possesses primal Being by its very nature will exist eternally.

This primal and eternal Being, therefore, cannot be dead, like a stone or wood, but must be living; and its life must be pure, to the extent that it remains transcendent. Its blending with inferior existence obstructs its access to the highest, yet cannot destroy its nature; and it may recover its 'ancient state'[3] by rising to its own.

iii) Soul's lowest phase, Nature, creates the world by contemplation
III 8.iv

If Nature were asked for what purpose it creates, and were willing to listen to the questioner and reply, it would say: 'You should not have asked, but understood in silence, just as I keep silence and make no habit of talking. What should you understand? That what comes into being is what I see in my silence, a vision naturally come to birth; and that I, sprung from such contemplation, am myself inherently contemplative. My consciousness creates its own vision, just as geometers draw figures while they study; but I do not draw, but as I look, the figures of material bodies come to be, as if falling from my consciousness. It is with me as with my Mother and the Beings that begot me, offspring themselves of contemplation. My birth is not by any act of theirs, those principles of higher ancestry, but as they contemplate themselves I come to birth.'

What, then, does this mean? That what we call Nature is Soul, child of a prior Soul more potently alive, a Soul at peace and in possession of an inner vision, with neither upward nor yet downward tendency, but reposing in its being, its own stillness and awareness of itself; and in this consciousness and self-awareness it beholds its own progeny, to the limit of its powers, and has no further aim than the noble and delightful spectacle it has perfected.

If it is desired to attribute understanding or perception to it, this will not be what is meant by understanding or perception elsewhere, but as if one should compare the mind of one sleeping with one awake. Nature is at rest in contemplation of the vision of itself, a vision present to it by virtue of its self-contained unity of being as object for itself. Its contemplation is silent, but somewhat faint; for there exists another, clearer to behold, and Nature is the image of another contemplation. Everything born of Nature, therefore, is weak, because weak contemplation creates a weak object of vision.

In the same way, when the power of contemplation is weak in men, they find a shadow of contemplation and thought in the life of action. Through weakness of soul they find no satisfaction in the life of contemplation, and are unfulfilled, failing to grasp the vision adequately; yet in their desire to see they take to action, to see there what with their intellect they cannot see. Whatever they achieve, when purpose is successfully realised in action, they want to see and contemplate themselves, and bring before the notice of all others. Everywhere we shall find that making and action are either a weakening or an accompaniment of contemplation: a weakening, if the doer has no vision beyond the act itself; an accompaniment, if he has a prior object of contemplation, superior to the work produced.

Who, if capable of contemplating Reality, prefers to pursue the image of Reality? Children of dull intelligence bear witness to this, in that, incapable of intellectual and theoretical study, they descend to the crafts and manual labour.

iv) The ensoulment of the universe

IV 3.ix

We must also enquire how soul comes to inhabit body. In what manner does it enter? This is a question well worth our interest and investigation.

The entry of soul into body takes place in two ways. Firstly, a soul already present in body may change bodies, or a soul may pass from an aerial or fiery body into one of earth - which is not described as a change of body since its earlier habitation is not apparent. Secondly, there is its entry from a wholly bodiless state into any kind of body, which will clearly be soul's first communion with body. This is an important subject for investigation: what actually happens when a soul utterly pure of body takes upon itself a bodily nature?

It is perhaps reasonable, or rather, necessary, to begin with the Soul of the Universe; and it should be understood that our argument talks of the 'entry' of soul and of 'ensouling' only for clarity of explanation. For there was never a time when this Universe was not ensouled, or when body existed in the absence of soul, or when matter was unordered; but we may separate these things conceptually for the purpose of argument. Any composite whole may be analysed into its parts to facilitate rational exposition.

The truth is as follows. If body did not exist, there would be no procession of soul, as there is no other natural habitation for it. If it is to go forth, it will beget a place for itself, and so beget body. Soul's place of rest is established, so to say, in absolute Rest, from which a great light shines; and at the furthest limits of this blaze there is a darkness, a substrate unformed, which soul sees and brings to shape. It is not in the law of things that any neighbour of soul should be without a share in formative Reason, as far as that may which merits description as the dark within the darkness.

It is as if a beautiful and richly varied mansion comes into being, which its creator does not desert, nor yet inhabit; rather, he considers it worthy of his care in every part, a care that sustains its being – as far as it can partake of being – and its beauty, yet with no impairment to its master, who presides from on high. In such a way is the universe ensouled, by a soul not its own but imparted to it, mastered and not mastering, possessed and not possessing. For the world lies in soul, which bears it up, and there is nothing without a share in soul.

It is as if a net were alive and soaked in water, but unable to gain possession of the element that contains it; as the sea extends, so the net extends with it as far as it may, for no one of its parts can wander from its place. Soul's nature is so great, because without magnitude, as to comprehend all body in its grasp, and wherever body extends, there is soul. If body did not exist, soul would not be affected in respect of magnitude; it is what it is. For the universe extends as far as the presence of soul, and the limit of its advance lies within soul's sustaining power. The shadow is as wide as the scope of soul's creative Reason, and the power of Reason such as to create whatever magnitude the Divine Reality intends.

v) The life of Soul in movement constitutes Time
III 7.xi

We must go back to that state which we affirmed of Eternity, that untroubled life, still concentrated, unbounded, without any declension, set in unity and towards unity. Time did not yet exist, or at least not for those eternal beings; we shall bring Time to birth in the creative operation of the nature that succeeds them. While the Intelligible world, then, was at rest in itself, one could hardly summon the Muses, who did not yet exist, to tell 'how Time first fell out'; but, even if the Muses existed, one might perhaps ask Time itself, after its birth, how it was revealed and came into being. And it would speak of itself somewhat as follows.

Formerly, that is to say, when it had not yet generated this 'formerly' or had need of 'later', it reposed with Eternity in real Being; it was not Time, but itself was at rest in Eternity. But there was a restless nature that desired self-rule and independence, and coveted more than it owned, and when it stirred, then Time also stirred; and moving always towards the future and the later, identity replaced by ever-changing succession, we lengthened out our journey and fashioned Time as an image of Eternity.

Soul possessed an unquiet faculty, and was for ever wishing to transfer elsewhere its higher vision; it was unwilling to possess it in its concentrated fullness. And, just as from a still seed the informing principle unfolds itself and develops, as it seems, to greater magnitude, yet by division its magnitude is cancelled, and it loses strength as it extends, no longer self-contained in unity but spending its unity beyond itself; in the same way Soul, in creating the world of sense in imitation of that higher world, moving not with the movement of the Divine, but with a semblance of it, in desire to copy it, firstly took Time upon itself in substitution for Eternity, then gave the world to be Time's slave, assigning it wholly to Time and conjoining all its ways in Time. For as the world moves in Soul, there being no place for all this Universe but Soul, it moves also in the Time of Soul.

Soul acts in successive moments, an unending sequence, and with its activity begets succession; it progresses, as it follows thought with thought, to what formerly did not exist, when thinking was not activitated and its life was unlike the present. There is at once a difference of life, therefore, and the difference involves a difference of Time. The successive intervals of life constitute Time, the continuous advance of life constitutes the indefinite extension of Time, and life past constitutes past Time.

So would it be right to define Time as the life of the Soul in movement as it passes from one stage of living to another? Yes, for if Eternity is life at rest, unchanging, identical and unbounded, and if Time must be an image of Eternity, like this universe in relation to that higher reality; then we must say that, corresponding to the life There, there must be another life synonymous with this power of the Soul; and corresponding to the movement of the Intelligible, there is movement of a part of Soul; and instead of the identity and unchangeableness of what remains, there is the impermanence of successive action; instead of unextended unity, there is the unity of continuous sequence, an image of unity; instead of reality whole and unbounded in an eternal present, there is indefinite and unending futurity; and instead of a concentrated totality, a totality for ever unfolding in part. Only by seeking always to extend its being will Time be an image of Eternity, the entire, concentrated and unbounded; for only so will it mirror the essence of the Intelligible.

We must not suppose Time to be outside Soul, just as Eternity is not outside real Being; nor again is it an accompaniment or successor of Soul, any more than Eternity in its sphere. It is visible in Soul, inherent in Soul, co-existent with Soul, like Eternity in the Intelligible.

vi) Soul is present everywhere in its entirety
VI 4.xii

Often, when a voice sounds in the air and speech is carried in the voice, an ear close by catches and perceives it, and the speech and the voice would reach any other ear interposed in the space between, or rather, the ear would reach out to the speech; and similarly, many eyes look in the same direction and all are filled with the sight, though the object of sight is separate because of the difference between the organs. In just the same way, what is capable of ensoulment will possess itself of soul, and again another and another will draw from the same source.

The voice occupied all the air, not as one fragmented but as one everywhere entire; and so with the object of sight, if the air bears the shape of its impress, it bears it undivided; for wherever the eye is placed, there it receives the shape. This theory of vision is not universally held, but it is adequate witness of participation in an identical unity. The example of the voice shows more clearly how form can pervade the whole air in its entirety; for everyone would not have heard the same unless the spoken word had been entire in every place, for each ear alike to catch the whole.

Now if even in this world of sense the sound of the voice can be diffused through the whole air, all undivided and with no fragmentary contact, why should we doubt that Soul in its unity is not extended by fragmentation into bodies, but is entirely present where it is present, and omnipresent and undivided throughout the universe? Upon becoming embodied, it will be like the voice already sounded in the air, but before its entry like the speaker on the point of utterance; and yet even when embodied it retains the character of the speaker, who in speaking both owns the voice and gives it. Our example of the voice may be an inexact analogy, but there is some resemblance; and we must understand that, as soul belongs to that other mode of Being, it is not embodied in part and part segregated, but is entire within itself beneath the semblance of multiplicity.

vii) The ensoulment of bodies is both spontaneous and necessary
IV 3.xiii

There is an ineluctable and natural Law which compels each existent to move in due order to that to which it individually tends, as the image of its primal choice and disposition; and every form of soul in that higher world is close to that sensible image to which its constitution conforms. It needs none, therefore, to send it at a specific time into body, and none to guide it to a particular body, but when its moment comes descends spontaneously and enters where it must. Each has its own time, and when that time arrives, like the summons of a herald, it descends and enters the body suited to it, as if the process were set in motion and maintained by magical powers or mysterious forces of compulsion. It is like the way in which soul perfects the development of every living creature, stirring each feature at its proper time and bringing it into being – the growth of beards and horns, for instance, and specific impulses, and new blossoming, and the development of trees through predetermined stages.

Souls go forth neither by free will nor by being sent; at least, their freedom is not deliberate choice, but like a natural leap, instinctive desire for sexual congress, or the uncalculating aspiration to noble deeds. Each is eternally destined to its own kind, and for each there is its proper time. The Mind which is before the universe has its own destiny, to remain on high whatever it sends forth, and the particular is sent forth by law, in obedience to the universal. The universal is contained in each particular, and it is by no external power that the Law brings things to their accomplishment: that strength is inherent in those that obey it, and they bear it around with them. At the moment appointed the Law's will is accomplished by those that possess it; it is they who bear the Law and they who fulfil it, made strong by its residing within them; and it weighs on them, implanting pains of labour and a longing to go where the Law within them summons.

viii) Souls fall away from God by self-will

V 1.i

What is it that has caused souls to forget God, their Father, and though members of that higher world and wholly subject to him, to become ignorant of themselves and of him?

The beginning of their misfortune was self-will, their genesis and first differentiation from their source, their desire to own themselves. Displaying delight in their independence, they moved freely as they willed, running against nature and straying far from their origin, till they forgot their divine parentage. They were like children, torn from their parents at birth and for many years brought up far away, who forget their own and their parents' identity. Unable any more to see God or themselves, in dishonour of self and ignorance of their ancestry, they gave honour to everything more than themselves, and all their wonder and awe and respect was for these others; and dependent on these they broke loose, as far as soul may, in disdain of that Father they deserted. The cause, therefore, of their utter ignorance of God is their knowing this world of sense and dishonouring themselves.

What pursues and admires another admits its own inferiority; and what accepts a lower place than things of transitory existence, reckoning itself less worthy and enduring than all that it admires, could entertain no notion of the nature and power of God. To those in this condition, therefore, there is need of a double argument to turn them round towards their origin, and lead them up to that Highest, One and First.

What are these two arguments? One, which shows the dishonour of what the soul now honours, we shall elaborate more fully elsewhere; but the other, which teaches and reminds the soul of its high ancestry and worth, is prior to the other, and when made explicit will serve for both. Of this we must now speak.

ix) Every soul is one with the World Soul

V 1.ii

Let every soul, then, reflect first on this, that it made all living things itself, breathing life into them, both those that the earth and those that the sea nourishes, and the creatures of the air and the divine stars in the heaven; and that it made the sun and made this great heaven, and itself adorned it and itself drives it round in its appointed motion. Yet soul is of a different nature from what it orders and moves and brings to life, and its worth must be greater than theirs; for they come to birth or perish as soul bestows life or abandons them, while soul, since 'it does not abandon itself',[4] exists eternally.

As to the manner of its bestowing life to the whole and each part, let soul reason thus. Let it observe the great Soul, as a soul itself made precious and worthy of the sight, freed from deceit and the distractions that beguile other souls, in utter stillness. Still be the body that envelops it, and the body's surging sea, and all that surrounds it; still the earth, still the sea and the air, and the heaven itself at peace. Let it imagine, in that repose, Soul flowing from outside into this heaven, pouring and entering in at every point, and flooding it with light; for just as the sun's rays illumine a dark cloud and make it gleam like gold, so does Soul, on entering heaven's body, give it life and immortality, and awakens what lies dead. And heaven, moved in everlasting motion by the rational power of Soul, becomes a living and blessed being, and gains honour as Soul's dwelling-place; which yet before Soul entered it was dead body, earth and water, or darkness of matter, rather, and non-being, a thing 'hateful to the gods', as the poet says.

The power and nature of Soul will become more clearly evident if we consider how it encompasses the heaven and guides it according to its will. To all this vast expanse, as far as it extends, it gives itself, and every interval, both large and small, is filled with Soul. Bodies are located separately, each with its own form, some in opposition and others set apart in other ways; but it is not so with Soul. Soul enlivens all things with its whole self, not each separate body with a fragment of Soul, and all Soul is present everywhere, like the Father who begat it in its omnipresent unity. And vast and diversified though this universe is, it is one by the power of Soul and a god because of Soul. The sun also is a god, because ensouled, and the other stars, and if we ourselves partake of the Divine, this is the cause: for 'dead bodies are viler than dung'.[5]

The principle by which the gods are gods must be an older god than they. Our soul also is of the same form, and when you take it and observe it purified of its accretions, you will find that same precious nature that we said was Soul, and more precious than all material existence.

REFERENCES

1. Plato, *Timaeus*, 25a.
2. Plato, *Phaedrus*, 245 c9.
3. Plato, *Republic*, 547b 6–7.
4. Plato, *Phaedrus*, 245 c9.
5. Heraclitus, *Diels*, B 96.

IV

Matter and Evil

Summary

i) The important distinction between potentiality and actuality, which Aristotle uses in accounting for generation and change in the physical world, is applied by Plotinus, in his own way, to the explanation of the nature of the Matter of the sensible world. Matter is absolute potentiality, unmodified by the forms that it reflects, and therefore strictly non-existent.

ii) As against Aristotle, Plotinus insists that Matter is utter privation, unaffected by form, and that forms in matter are 'mere images of intelligible beings'. Phrases like 'small and large' are borrowed from the Platonic-Pythagorean description of the Indefinite Dyad. The lower matter of the sensible world is itself a poor image of the intelligible matter that is perfectly adapted to the forms of intelligible beings. There is no privation within Being.

iii) This passage shows that Matter plays a necessary, if not entirely convincing, role in Plotinus' metaphysics as the source of Evil; it is even called, rhetorically, 'absolute Evil', but in a world generated by the Good there can be no independent Principle of Evil.

iv) This extract presents a strongly positive valuation of Matter: a creature of the Good, it is necessary for the expression of the Good in the visible universe. The metaphor of the unfolding seed here suggests an almost evolutionary view of creation.

i) Matter, as universal potentiality, is strictly non-existent

II 5.iv

Everything else that is potentially something particular has its actual existence as some other thing; it already exists, and is said to exist potentially in relation to another. But as regards Matter, which is said to exist, and which we describe as potentially everything that exists, how can it be said to be actually something existent? If it were, it would no longer be potentially everything that exists. So if it is nothing existent, it must be non-existent.

How then, could it be something in actuality if it is nothing existent? It might not be any of those things whose existence is formed upon Matter, yet nothing prevents it from being something else, since Matter does not underlie all that exists. In so far, then, as it is none of the things formed upon Matter, and these have existence, it will be non-existent.

Since it is conceived of as something formless, it will not be a form, and cannot, therefore, be classed among the Intelligibles. In this respect also, it will be non-existent, and its non-existence in both worlds makes it the more non-existent. It is too elusive, therefore, to have the character of authentic existence, and it cannot attain either to the status of fictional existence, being not even a phantom of rational form, as fictions are.

Under what mode of existence, then, can it be grasped? And if under no mode of existence, what could it actually be?

II 5.v

What is our account of it? How is it the matter of things that exist?

It is they potentially. Then, because it is already they potentially, it is not now as it is to become; its existence is merely the announcement of its future, as if existence is deferred for it until its future state. Its potential existence, therefore, is not as something particular, but as potentially everything; and as it is nothing in itself, beyond what it is as Matter, it has no actual existence either. For if it were something actually, it would be actually not Matter, but the particular actualisation, and therefore not Matter absolutely, but only in the sense in which bronze is the matter of the statue.

It will be non-existent, then, and not in the sense of being different from existence, like motion; for motion accompanies existence, derived from it and contained in it, whereas Matter is an outcast, absolutely segregated and without power to change itself, always retaining its original nature of non-existence. Divorced from all real beings, it had no actual existence in the beginning, nor did it attain to actuality; for from the realities under which it chooses to hide it has acquired not a tinge of colour, but is always in wait for another, potentiality to successive realities. Only when the procession of real beings ceased, did it appear, and it occupies last place, behind even these later existents that laid hold on it.

Grasped, then, by both orders of existence, it can belong to neither in actuality; its fate is to be potentiality merely, a feeble and faint shadow with no power to take on form. It is therefore actually a shadow, and so actually a falsity; which is equivalent to 'true falsity',[1] or 'real non-existence'.[2]

ii) The unreality and impassibility of Matter
III 6.vii

It is an image and phantom of corporeal mass, a mere tendency to substantial existence, static but without position; it is invisible in itself, eluding all attempts to observe it, present yet unseen, however intent the gaze; and it for ever wears contrary appearances, small and large, less and more, deficient and excessive, a phantom that neither remains nor yet can escape, so absolute is its weakness. Entirely devoid of Being, it has inherited no strength from Mind.

Its every proclamation is a lie; if it appears large, it is small, if more, less; its semblance of Being is no Being, but a fleeting trick, and all the forms it seems to hold are tricks, nothing but phantoms in a phantom, like a reflection in a mirror that appears where it is not. It appears filled and possessed of everything; yet it is empty. 'Images of intelligible beings pass in and out of it',[3] ghosts into a formless ghost, visible by its very formlessness. They seem to act on it, but without effect, weak and insubstantial phantoms; they carry no force, and matter gives no resistance; they pass through without cutting, as if through water, or like shapes floating through the Void.

If the forms visible in matter were of a kind with their originals, they might be credited with some power from that source which would modify matter on their entry; but as it is, the appearances are of a different order from the realities reflected in them, and prove the falsity of the affection, where the visible form is a lie and wholly dissimilar to its formal cause. Feeble and false, and descending into falsity, like an image in a dream, or water or a mirror, it leaves matter unaffected, of necessity; and more surely so than even in these analogies, where image and its cause are similar.

iii) Absolute Evil is Matter

I 8.ii

Intellect is the first act of the Good and the primal form of Being, and while the Good remains at the still centre, Intellect is active and alive around him. Beyond Intellect there revolves Soul, its gaze fixed upon it, and in seeing into the depths of Intellect it beholds God through it. This is the life of gods, untroubled and blessed, and evil has no place here; and if this were all, there would be no evil, but only a First Good and second and third goods. 'All things are about the King of all, and he is the cause of all good things, and all things are for his sake; and the second is about the second things and the third about the third things.'[4]

If these, therefore, are Being and what transcends Being, then evil will not be found in Being or the One that transcends Being; for these are good. It remains, then, if evil exists, that it exists in non-being, like a form of non-being, and belongs to what is blended with, or in some way partakes of, non-being. By 'non-being' I do not mean absolute non-being, but only something different from Being: not non-being in the sense of movement or rest, which accompany Being, but as a kind of image of Being, or non-being in an even remoter sense.

Such is the whole world of sense and all experience of the senses, or whatever is consequent upon or accidental to it, or its source, or any one of the elements of which this world of non-being consists. Evil might now be conceived of as measurelessness in contrast to measure, limitlessness in contrast to limit, formlessness in contrast to the formative, and perpetual deficiency in contrast to self-sufficiency; for ever undefined, nowhere steady, utterly impressionable, insatiable, absolute poverty. And all this is not accidental to it, but as it were its essence, and there is no part of it but has this character; and whatever partakes of it and is assimilated becomes evil, though not absolute evil.

In what mode of existence, then, are all these characteristics found, not as accidental to it but as its very self? For if evil can be an attribute of another, it must have some prior existence in itself, even if not that of real Being. Just as there is both absolute Good and good as an attribute, so there is both absolute Evil and the evil dependent on it which is attributed to another.

Where is measurelessness, if not in the unmeasured? Yet what of the Measure that is not in the measured? Just as there is Measure which is not in the measured, so there is Measurelessness which is not in the unmeasured. For if Measurelessness has no independent existence, it is either in the unmeasured or in the measured; yet the unmeasured has no need of it, while the measured, *qua* measured, has no room for measurelessness. There must, therefore, be something absolutely without limit and form, and with all the qualities mentioned above as characterising the nature of Evil; and whatever evil is derived from it, is evil either by blending with it or by attending to it or by producing such evils.

It is the substrate which underlies figures, forms, shapes, measures and limits, submitting itself to extraneous ordering, possessing no good of itself, a mere shadow in relation to real Being, the very essence of Evil, if such is possible. This it is that our argument discovers to be the primal Evil and absolute Evil.

iv) Even Matter, at the limit of creation, shares in the Good
IV 8.vi

It cannot be that One only should exist, or all would lie buried in him, without Form, and none of the intelligible beings would exist, had he remained self-contained and static; nor would there be plurality of forms begotten by the One without the procession of souls, which hold the next rank. Similarly, the creative process cannot end with souls: their offspring must arise, if to each kind belongs a natural impulse to generate its successor.

The process is like the unfolding of a seed, moving from simple origin to termination in the world of sense, the prior always remaining in its place, while begetting its successor from a store of indescribable power - power that must not halt within the higher realm, as if circumscribed by jealousy, but continue to expand until the universe of things reaches the limit of its possibility, lavishing its vast resource on all its creatures, intolerant that any one should have no share in it. Nothing is debarred from participation in the Good, to the extent of its receptivity.

Matter, therefore, if it always existed, could not but share in that Source that bestows Good on its creatures, universally and to the capacity of each; and if it came to birth of necessity as a consequent of prior causes, not even so could it be excluded from the Good. For he who brought it to existence in his gift could not withhold himself through failing power.

The greatest beauty, therefore, in the world of sense reflects the nobility of intelligible beings, and their power and goodness, and all existence is for ever interlinked, forms of pure Being with objects of sense; the higher realities self-caused, the lower living in dependence on them, as participants in, and images of the Intelligible, to the capacity of their material nature.

REFERENCES

1. Plato, *Republic*, 382 a4.
2. Plato, *Sophist*, 254 d1.
3. Plato, *Timaeus*, 50 c4-5.
4. Plato, *Letter II*, 312 e1-4.

V

The Material Universe

Summary

i) A protest against any account of Creation which implies conscious planning.

The description of matter as 'form' is remarkable.

ii) The belief that the celestial gods, perfect and unchanging as they are, deliberately interfere in the events of earth has been dismissed as absurd; but Plotinus accepts the possibility of astrological predictions and the efficacy of human prayer and magic, attributing them to the natural sympathy by which Soul binds the whole universe.

'Partial membership' of the material universe is the condition of man, whose higher soul lives in the realm of pure Being.

The essential point, of spontaneous but inevitable harmony, is effectively illustrated by the image of the dancer. The solo 'pantomimus', dancing a story from mythology to the accompaniment of instruments and chorus, was a popular entertainer in ancient Rome.

iii) Just as in the individual man the higher soul is unaffected by magic charms, so the celestial gods pay no conscious attention to prayer: their responses are but one example of the universal sympathy.

iv) Conflict is a necessary consequence of the diversity of the material universe and the imperfection of its parts, but aesthetic analogies are used to show that the pattern of the whole may be good, under the direction of Providence and the divine Logos, and that it is always true that 'unity results, even if composed of opposites'.

Our own actions are not predetermined, but our choices themselves can only contribute to the providential order. Plotinus adheres to the Socratic principle that no one does wrong willingly, but only in ignorance, yet upholds blame and punishment for wickedness as responses required by providential Reason.

In answer to his concluding question, Plotinus reasserts the necessity of opposition in a manifold universe, and distinguishes Fate, operative here below, from a higher Providence which ensures that 'virtue is everywhere in control' (III 3.v). True freedom in man, it will be argued, exists only in the life of intellect.

v) In denunciation of the dualism, typical of Gnosticism, which regards the material universe, including the celestial gods, as evil and created in error, Plotinus concludes with an emotional appeal to the grandeur of the visible world.

vi) A refutation of the 'commonsense' opinion that material objects are what are most real, and that our perception of them is our contact with reality.

The soul, the incorporeal source of life and movement, is wholly immune to affections and indestructible; in the material world its closest neighbour is fire, treated by Plotinus as an intermediary between spiritual and material existence.

In the concluding sentences, there is a possible criticism of the Christian doctrine of the resurrection of the body.

i) The material Universe is an image of the Intelligible, and unplanned
V 8.vii

As to this universe, we are agreed that its existence and nature are derived from another. Are we to suppose, then, that its creator formed a conception of earth, determining its position in the centre, and then of water, and its position as lying upon the earth, and of all else in order as far as the heaven; and that he then conceived all living creatures, each with its present shape, its inward organs and outward limbs; and that only then, every detail arranged in his mind, he set about his work?

No such conception was possible - for how could it occur to one who had never had sight of it? Nor could he have realised a borrowed plan in the way that craftsmen create, using hands and tools; for hands and feet are a later development. Only one possibility remains, therefore: all things exist in something else, and as no interval separates them, but all are continuous within the realm of Being, there suddenly appears a kind of apparition or image of that prior reality, whether projected directly or by the ministration of Soul, or of a particular soul - this matters not for our present purpose.

This universe in its totality is derived from the Intelligible, and There it exists in greater beauty; for here it is corrupted, but There incorrupt. It is composed of ideal forms from beginning to end, first Matter informed by the elements, then other forms upon these forms, then again further forms; so that Matter, concealed beneath manifold forms, is hard to detect. And since even Matter is form in the lowest degree, this whole universe is form, and all its parts are forms, as its archetype is form; and its creation is silent, effected by nothing but Being and Form. No toil, therefore, attends its construction.

ii) Sympathy pervades the entire living universe

IV 4.xxxii

If we cannot attribute to physical causes or to deliberate acts those external influences which reach to us from heaven, and to all living creatures and the whole earth, what reasonable explanation remains?

Firstly, we must affirm that this universe is 'a single living being embracing all living beings within it',[1] and possessing a single Soul that permeates all its parts to the degree of their participation in it; and that every part of this sensible universe is fully participant in its material aspect, and in respect of soul, in the degree to which it shares in the World Soul. Further, the parts informed by the World Soul alone are fully integrated in the whole, while those that participate also in another Soul have partial membership; yet all parts experience influence from the others, to the extent of their integration and in correspondence to their constituent elements.

A sympathy pervades this single universe, like a single living creature, and the distant is near; just as in an individual animal the nail, horn, finger or other limb are not contiguous, yet sensation occurs in the remoter part, leaving the intervening body unaffected. Like parts lie not in contact but separated, with other parts between, yet by their likeness they feel sympathy, and the action of a distant member is necessarily felt far off; and in a living and unified being there is no part so remote as not to be near, through the very nature that binds the living unity in sympathy.

IV 4.xxxiii

As the circuit of the universe is not random, but governed by the rational design of its living organism, there must exist a harmony between action and experience, and an order which arranges the parts in complementary relation with each other; and corresponding to each figure in the circuit, the things subject to the circuit must be differently disposed, as if executing a single dance through an intricate variety of movements.

Human dance is analogous. Its external features, flutes, singing and the other accompaniments that contribute to the dancing, change in response to each movement; and this is too obvious to need mention. But the dancer's body also necessarily changes position from one figure to another, as his limbs bend in following the dance, one bearing his weight, another relaxed, one working hard, another resting in the changing configuration. The dancer's intention looks elsewhere, while his limbs obey the sequence of the dance and serve the dance, and combine to perfect the whole. An authority on dance would say that a particular configuration determines the raising or bending or concealing or lowering of different limbs, and that the dancer makes no idle choice of these movements, but as he performs the sequence each part of him has its necessary position in the dance of the whole body.

This is the manner, therefore, in which we must say that the heavenly bodies act or give signs, or rather, that the whole universe lives its whole life, moving its great parts within itself and for ever changing their positions. As of a single living being in movement, the positions of the parts in relation to each other and the whole, and their different dispositions, cause all the lesser parts to follow, and to be variously arranged according to the varying positions, dispositions and configurations; so that it is not the elements in the pattern which are the actors, but their arranger. And again, the arranger is not an actor distinct from the material of his art, which is none other than himself: he himself is the sum of phenomena, the figures in the heavens and their consequences on earth, inevitable affections of the living being that moves in this way and is so constructed and conjoined by nature, a being at once agent and object of its own activity, by bonds of necessity.

iii) Magic and prayer are effective through the sympathy of the universe

IV 4.xl

Suppose a magician were outside the universe: he could not entice or bring down powers by bewitchments or binding spells. But as it is, because he operates from within the world, he makes his influence felt, knowing the mutual attractions at work within the living organism. There is a natural enchantment in spells, arising from the time, the character of the utterance, and the posture of the magician; such things attract, as pitiable gestures and cries attract. For it is not the deliberative and rational mind that is charmed by music, but the irrational soul, and such magic occasions no surprise; indeed, bewitchment is welcomed, even if not required of musicians.

Nor must we think that prayers of other kinds are heard and answered by deliberate will. People are not deliberately charmed by spells, and understanding and perception play no part in fascination by a snake; knowledge follows the experience, and the ruling intellect is unaffected. Prayer similarly brings down some influence from a heavenly body, whether upon the speaker or another.

IV 4.xli

But the sun or other star does not listen to his prayer. The prayer is answered by the sympathy of the universe, connecting part with part as in a single taut string, which if plucked at one end vibrates also at the other. Often, the plucking of one string is sensed by another, in harmony with it and tuned to a similar scale; and vibration can pass even from lyre to lyre, so great is the sympathy. In view of this, throughout the universe, though composed of contraries, a single harmony exists, and even those contraries share an affinity and kinship.

iv) Providence, evil, and man's responsibility

III 2.xvii

The rational principle of the universe is manifested in its creation, and the greater its diversity, the more contrasting will its productions be; and the world of sense, being less unified than its principle, will be more manifold and its elements more opposed, each with a stronger urge to live, a stronger desire to come to unity. Lovers, in seeking their good, often destroy the objects of their love, when these are perishable, and the yearning of the part for its fulfilment in the whole draws to it what it can in its career.

Thus both the good and the bad exist, like contrasting movements of a dancer obedient to the same art; and while we see both good and bad in the different sections of the dance, it is the contrast that gives perfection to the whole. Does this acquit the wicked of their wickedness? No, their wickedness is not cancelled, except that its origin lies not in themselves; and this might excuse them, but that forgiveness stems from the creative principle which forbids us to excuse the wicked.

Both good and bad - and the bad in greater numbers - are found among its creatures, just as in a play the author assigns roles to the actors while making use of their own characters; he does not himself rank them as leading actor and second and third, but by giving suitable words to each determines the place appropriate to him. Similarly, every man has his place, one fit for the good, another for the wicked; and each sort goes to his proper place, in conformity with nature and its rational principle, to occupy the position of his choice. Then one of them blasphemes and perpetrates crimes, the other does the opposite, like actors lending to the play the characters they were before.

In plays staged by men, the author supplies the words, while each of the actors determines, by his own talent and performance, the quality of his contribution – for they have more to do than merely recite the author's lines; but in the truer work of creation, which poetic talent in part imitates, it is soul that acts, its part assigned by the creator. The masks and costumes, saffron robes and rags worn by our actors here are counterparts of fortunes allotted to soul itself, not at random but by rational purpose, fortunes adapted to the plot through which the soul fits harmoniously into the grand design of the drama; and it then sings its song in actions and in all that a soul can do to display its character.

An actor's voice or posture will be as beautiful or ugly as he makes them, either enhancing the work, as expected, or if the voice be bad, detracting from his performance while leaving the drama's merit unaffected. Its author, like a good judge, dismisses him in deserved disgrace, finding him a part in some lesser play, while he promotes another to the place of honour and to parts in his finer plays. And so the soul, entering this drama of the universe and taking a part in the action, performs well or ill according to its disposition; assigned its place at the entrance, and given all but its own character and works, it is punished or rewarded.

But souls have an advantage in acting in a wider setting than the confines of a stage; their author makes them masters of this universe, with greater power to range, and determine their own honour or dishonour, according to their contribution. Each place they occupy is adapted to their characters, in keeping with the universal design, and each individual properly inserted into a receptive environment – just as each string of the lyre is set in order in its appropriate place, according to musical principle, to make its characteristic sound.

There is fitness and beauty in the whole when each holds his rightful place, even though it be to utter curses in the darkness of Tartarus; for such sounds there are beauty. This universe is beautiful, not because everyone is a Linus, but when each contributes his voice to the perfecting of a total harmony, a voice with life in its sound, however faint, subdued and imperfect. A pan-pipe, too, has more than one note, and even a faint, obscure sound helps to complete the pipe's full harmony; the harmony is composed of unequal notes, and every sound is at a different pitch, yet all combine to effect a completed unity. In the system of the universe even the ugliness in souls will count for beauty, their unnatural sounds conformable to the universal law of nature. Their sound will be none the less debased, yet the whole is in no way depreciated by its utterance. To use another image, even that sordid officer the executioner does not detract from a well-ordered state, for it has need of him, and such a man has many uses; so even he is well adapted.

III 2.xviii

Souls are better or worse from many causes, including their initial inequality; consistently with their creative principle, they are unequal parts by reason of their separation. And we must remember that a soul has its second and third phases and is not always active at the same level.

However, the other point of view needs stating, and further discussion is necessary to clarify the issue. There can be no question of introducing actors who speak lines not written by the author, as if his original drama were incomplete, with blank spaces in it, and they were supplying the missing content; for such actors would be no actors but a part of the poet, with foreknowledge of what they would say, and so able to connect all the parts in proper sequence. The creative principles in the universe link together evil deeds and their consequences in a rational design: from adultery and the enslavement of enemies, for example, nature may produce children to grow into a finer breed of men, and nobler cities may rise from the ruins of cities cruelly destroyed. It would be absurd, therefore, to introduce souls as responsible agents of good and evil, and if we acquit the rational design of responsibility for evils we can give it no credit for the good.

Why should we not reckon the deeds of the actors as parts of the ordered drama of the universe, like the parts in a play, attributing the good and evil in it, and the determination of each actor's role, to the creative principle? The greater perfection of the universal order, and the dependence of all things on that principle, give plausibility to the idea. But for what purpose does the principle cause evil to exist?

v) The beauty of the world of sense

II 9.xvi

What musician could there be who sees the harmony in the intelligible world and will not be stirred to hear the harmony in sensible sounds? What expert in geometry or arithmetic will not be delighted when his eyes encounter symmetry, proportion and order? In paintings, also, those who study the artistry with their eyes have different perceptions of the same work, and when they recognise a sensible representation of an idea in the mind they feel disturbed and are brought to recollection of the reality - an experience from which love arises.

But if the sight of beauty finely represented in a face can bear a man up to the higher reality, will there be any so dull-witted and unresponsive, in seeing all the varied beauty in the world of sense, in all its symmetry and ordered might, and the formal perfection displayed in the stars, for all their remoteness, that he will not stand in awe at it, reflecting on the glory from which such things derive? If so, he fails to understand this world and has never seen that other.

vi) The unreality of bodies

III 6.vi

How can physical objects like mountains, rocks and the whole solid earth, and the Matter which underlies them, be unreal? All that resists, all that exerts force on what it strikes, bears witness to their reality. And what if it be asked 'How can Soul and Intellect, which exert no pressure or force and offer no resistance, be called real, and real Being? And among material existents, how can the lighter and more mobile be more real than the unmoving earth, and the element above than this below? And how can fire, scarcely contained in bodily nature, be real?'

In my judgement, however, it is the more self-sufficient that bear less heavily and hurtfully on others, while the weightier and earthier bodies, deficient, falling and powerless to lift themselves, make impact as they fall through their inherent weakness, by the downward tendency of their inert mass. It is lifeless bodies that cause most pain, and inflict the most damaging blows, while ensouled bodies, in proportion as they partake of Being, are more kindly to their neighbours.

Movement is a sort of life in bodies, an imitation of life, and is most evident where there is least of body, a testimony that it is deficiency of Being that makes for corporeality. And consider what are called the affections: the greater the bodily constituent, the stronger the susceptibility to affections – strongest in earth and proportioned in the other elements by the same principle. The other elements, when separated, revert to unity unless held apart, but every earthly body, once severed, stays parted for ever. A failing of the natural powers prevents recovery from attack, and even a slight blow causes destruction; and just so, whatever consists most fully of body is furthest reduced to unreality, and too weak to regain its unity. Bodies destroy each other by the weight and force of their impact, weak falling upon weak and unreal upon unreal; and this is their only strength.

These are our arguments against those who locate reality in bodies, and who cite the evidence of the forces exerted by bodies, and the images provided by sense-perception, in confirmation of their view. They behave like dreamers, who think that the figments of their dreams really exist. Sense-perception belongs to the sleeping soul, the part of the soul immersed in body; and the true awakening is a rising up, not with the body, but from the body. To rise with the body is to shift from one sleep to another, as if changing beds, but to rise up in very truth is altogether to depart from bodies. Corporeality is contrary to soul and essentially opposed to soul, as testified by the birth, change and decay that bodies suffer, processes foreign to the nature of Being.

REFERENCE

1. Plato, *Timaeus*, 30 d3–31 a1.

VI
Man

Summary

i) The true self of each of us belongs eternally in Intellect, independent of the body, but we are not always aware of it. Our primal unity has been lost by the ensoulment of a particular body and the emergence of 'another man', the isolated embodied individual, from whom our task is to free ourselves.

ii) In the body, our self, strictly speaking, is our faculty of reason, not the lower soul of perception, emotion and appetite, and in discursive thought our mind has access to the intelligible truths eternally known by Intellect, with which our highest soul has kinship.

In perception, the sense-organs transmit impressions to the soul, which converts them into images; on these images, and with reference to the intelligible forms, the higher soul makes judgements about the external world.

iii) The Greek *eudaimonia* refers not to feelings of happiness but to a relatively permanent state of mind; but Aristotle tells us that it is universally agreed to be the aim of life. 'Happiness', therefore, is a reasonable, but not exact, translation.

Plotinus argues that happiness, as perfection of life, belongs to the life of intellect, and that therefore external circumstances and bodily experiences are irrelevant to it. It is characteristic of Neoplatonism to explain the meaning of 'life' as a graded series.

iv) In a number of noteworthy passages, Plotinus recognises the reality of unconscious sensations, desires and dispositions. Here he draws the logical, but paradoxical, conclusion that since we are often unconscious of our life in intellect, consciousness is not necessary to happiness. It seems that we are happy all the time, therefore, but only the sage is aware of his happiness.

v) Happiness, as defined, belongs in eternity, not the life of temporal process.

vi) Moral virtue is the imposition of order and measure on bodily desires and emotions; it is, therefore, specifically as the Indeterminate that Matter causes vice and delusions in the soul.

vii) Plotinus is concerned to reconcile two attitudes to the descent of the individual soul which occur in Plato's dialogues: on the one hand, the body is the tomb or cave in which the soul is imprisoned, on the other, the soul is sent by god to perfect the visible world in the image of the intelligible.

Descent as such is both a decline and a necessary fulfilment of the law of creation. The descended soul has then to choose what attitude to adopt to the embodied state, whether to exploit it for good or to be enslaved.

viii) Plotinus adapts Aristotle's analysis of voluntary action as action, unconstrained, in full knowledge of the right and of relevant circumstances. He goes on to argue that complete freedom is therefore impossible for the embodied soul: only intellect is truly free, in being directed towards the Good. True freedom is to desire to do what one ought to do, not to be able to do whatever one desires.

ix) These words, the last in the *Enneads* that Plotinus wrote before his own death, declare the superiority of death over life in the body, the good life itself being withdrawal from the body.

x) In the pursuit of true happiness, the body is dispensable, but not contemptible.

i) The birth of Man

VI 4.xiv

The realm of the Intelligible is that of primeval and original Being, the world of Becoming an approximation, an apprehension of Being, a dependence on Being.

And we – who are we? Do we belong to Being, or are we the child of Time, dependent on Being? Even before our birth here below, we existed There, men of another sort, as individuals and as gods, pure souls and intellect in union with universal Being, parts of the Intelligible not set apart or severed, but integral to the whole; for even now we are not cut off from it. But another man, craving existence, has now approached that primal Man, and finding us within the All, has enveloped us and encumbered the Man that was formerly the true self of each of us. It was as if a single voice sounded, bearing a single word, to which many lent their ears in different places so as to hear and receive it, so that hearing was made actual by the presence of its stimulus. We have become the dual Man, losing that former singleness, and on occasions the intruder only, while the primal self lies dormant or otherwise absents himself.

VI 4.xv

But how has the intruder made its approach? It had a natural bent, and laid hold of what was conformable to it; and its nature was adapted to receive soul. But whatever is incapable of receiving soul in its entirety – soul which is omnipresent, though not for it – like all other animals and plants, partakes as far as it may; just as at the utterance of a word, some grasp the meaning with the sound of the voice, while on others only the sound impinges. When, therefore, a living being comes to exist, compounded of both soul from the realm of Being, its link with all Being, and body, not empty or bereft of soul, but already ensouled; then body draws nearer, as if by natural bent, becoming no longer body only, but living body, and by proximity acquires a trace of soul - not a fragment of soul, but a kind of warming or radiance emitted by soul. This is the genesis of desire, and of pleasure and pain; and the living being comes to birth with a body not alien to it.

The soul sprung from the Divine lay still and self-grounded, true to its character; but the body, all confused and in flux through its weakness, and pounded by blows from without, begins itself to rail at the living union and impart its own turmoil to the whole.

In just such a way, when elders of the people sit in quiet reflection, the unruly crowd, demanding food and voicing other grievances, may throw their whole council into ugly confusion. Now if such people hold their peace, and a word from one of good sense gets to their ears, then order and moderation are restored and the worse element fails to gain the mastery; but otherwise the worse prevail while the better part keeps silent, because the rabble could not hear the word from on high. This, the vice of states and their councils, is also the vice of man, who possesses in himself a crowd of pleasures and desires and fears, which gain the mastery if the lower man surrenders to them.

Whoever brings that rabble to subjection, and reverts to that higher man he once was, lives that higher life and is that higher man, making concession to the body as to something distinct from self; while another, rising and falling back by turns, sullies his good self with the alien evil.

ii) The true self of man is his rational and intellectual soul

I 1.vii

Let us say that it is the complex of soul and body that has perception, and that the soul by its presence does not give itself as it is to the complex or its other member, but creates a distinct entity, combining the determinate nature of the body and a kind of light bestowed by soul according to the nature of the animal; and it is this complex creature to which perception and all other experiences of animate nature are attributed.

But how is it we who perceive? It is because we are not separate from the living being so constituted, even if other more precious elements go to make up the whole multifarious essence of Man. The soul's power of perception must not be of sensible objects, but rather, it must be able to apprehend impressions produced by sensation in the living being; for these are already intelligible entities. External sensation, then, is an image of this inner apprehension of the soul, which has the greater reality as being an impassive contemplation of pure forms. It is these forms, the source of soul's sovereignty over the living being, that make possible discursive reasoning, judgements and acts of intellect; and it is precisely here that 'we' are located. What is below this level of functioning belongs to us, but 'we' are the higher self that controls the whole complex being. There is no reason not to use the term 'living being' of the whole, while recognising that the true man rises above that lower, compounded part, which Plato calls the 'leonine' and the 'many-headed beast'.[1] For man coincides with the reasoning soul, so that when we reason it is 'we' who reason, since reasoning is an activity of soul.

I 1.viii

How are we related to Intellect? By 'Intellect' I mean, not that disposition of the soul that derives from Intellect, but Intellect itself.

We possess this also as something that transcends us, either as the common possession of us all or as particular to each, or else both common and particular – common, because undivided, a unity and everywhere identical; but particular, because each of us possesses Intellect in its totality in the highest part of his soul. We therefore contain within us the ideal forms of Being, and in two manifestations: in our soul, as it were unfolded and separated; and in Intellect, all in a unity.

iii) The nature of Happiness

I 4.iii

Let me explain my conception of happiness from the beginning, and make the assumption that happiness is a quality of life.

The word 'life' is used in many ways, with a different application according to the degree of existence, whether primal, or secondary, or another; and although 'living' is predicated of plants and irrational animals, it is used differently according to the brightness or dimness of the life of each. Clearly, this is equally true of living well; and where one is image of another, evidently the good life for it will be an image of a higher good.

Now if happiness belongs to whatever enjoys fullness of life, or, in other words, has no deficiency of life, then to live life fully, and nothing else, constitutes happiness; for only thus is excellence attained, if excellence among real existents is authentic life, or perfection of life, life not adventitiously good, and established in goodness on no accidental ground. What could be added to perfect life to bring it to excellence? If anyone answers 'the Absolute Good', the phrase is ours, but our search is not for the cause, but the essential constituent.

We have often said that the perfect, the real and authentic life is lived in the sphere of Intellect, and that all other lives are imperfect, mere images of life, not life complete and pure, and no more life than its contrary; and let it now be said concisely that, as long as all living things proceed from a single source, but have life to a lesser degree, then that principle must be the primary and most perfect life.

I 4.iv

If man is capable of the perfect life, then the man who enjoys such a life is happy; otherwise, perfection of life would be confined to the gods, and only they could be called happy. But since our claim is that men also may attain this happiness, we must consider how this can be. My view is as follows.

It has been shown elsewhere that man attains to the perfect life by his possession not only of sensation but of the power of reason and the authentic command of intellect. But are these powers alien to his humanity? No, any human being possesses them, either potentially or actually, and we affirm that they constitute his happiness. Shall we call this perfect form of life a part of the whole man? We hold, rather, that whereas in other men, possessing this life potentially, it plays a partial role; the happy man, in whom this form of life is actualised, has attained to that perfection in complete identity. All else is mere trappings now, unwanted and attached against his will, and so no proper part of him.

For such a man, then, what is good? He is his own good, by what he has; and the cause of good in him is Good itself, transcendent yet also immanent in man. That such a man seeks nothing else is testimony to his perfection: for what should he seek? Nothing of lesser worth, when united with the best. He who enjoys this life has all he needs, and the sage is self-sufficient for both happiness and possession of the good; there is no good that he does not own. Whatever else he seeks, he seeks as a necessity, not for himself but for the body attached to him, a body alive indeed, but living its own life, not the life of the sage. He knows its needs, and gives it what he gives without diminution of the life proper to him.

Even in adversities, therefore, his happiness will suffer no impairment; the good life endures through all. At the death of family or friends, he knows what death is, as do the victims if they are wise; and pain caused by their death hurt not the man's true self, but his unthinking part, whose sorrows he will not acknowledge.

I 4.vii

What circumstance of human life could be so grave as not to be despised by one who has risen above all earthly concerns, and broken all ties with the world below? For why should he who regards good fortune, however great, as of little moment – whether it be kingly power or rule over cities and peoples, or the founding of colonies and cities, even though he be the founder – stand in awe of the overthrow of rulers or the razing of his city? If he supposed such things a great evil, or an evil at all, he would surely be no sage but a fool, to set great store by timbers and stones and even, by Zeus, the deaths of mortal men; for he must hold death, we maintain, as preferable to life in the body. If he is offered in sacrifice, shall he think his death an evil because he died by the altars? If he goes unburied, his body will rot nonetheless, whether above the earth or beneath it. If he is buried with no costly ceremony, and without a name, lacking the honour of a lofty monument, what pettiness to resent it! Should he be led into captivity, there is a way of escape if happiness is impossible. And suppose his family were taken prisoner – 'his sons' wives and his daughters dragged off':[2] what if he died without seeing such a wrong? Would he depart in the belief that such things could not happen? Only a fool would think so. He would surely accept that such a fate might befall his own family – but will his belief in its possibility destroy his happiness? No, he remains happy in spite of it; and the fact of its happening, therefore, leaves him equally unmoved. He will reflect that this universe is so constituted as to bring such things to pass, and man must be resigned to it.

iv) Even consciousness is not necessary to Happiness

I 4.ix

But what if he loses consciousness, his mind drowned by sickness or magic arts? If it is allowed that he remains a sage in this state, though sunk in a kind of sleep, what prevents him being happy? No one denies him happiness during his sleep, and no one reckons up his hours of sleep to subtract them from the sum of his life's happiness; and if any refuse him the title of sage in this condition, then their argument no longer touches the sage. We presuppose a sage, and ask if his happiness endures as long as he lives in that life.

'Well, let him be a sage,' they say; 'without awareness, and without realising his virtue in act, but can he be happy?'

But he may be unaware of being healthy, or handsome, yet be nonetheless healthy or handsome for that; and if he is unaware that he is wise, will he be any the less wise?

It may be objected that wisdom demands the presence of conscious awareness, and that happiness resides in wisdom that is actualised.

Now if understanding and wisdom were adventitious, perhaps this argument would have some weight. But if wisdom, essentially, inheres in a real being, or rather, in Being itself, and this reality is not destroyed in sleep or in any state called unconscious; and if its activity continues in him, and is a sleepless activity; then even when unconscious, the sage will still be active as the sage. Not the whole man, but only a part of him, will remain ignorant of this activity; just as when growth is active in us, no apprehension of this activity reaches the rest of the man through the faculty of sense, and if we were our principle of growth, it would be we who were active even so. But as it is, we are not our vegetal life, but the activity of intellect; so that when intellect is active, we are active.

I 4.x

Perhaps this escapes us because intellect is not concerned with objects of sense; the mind seems to be active in relation to sensible objects through the mediation of sense-perception. But why should not intellect be active by itself, and the part of the soul that is akin to it, which is prior to sensation and all awareness? There must be act prior to awareness, if 'thinking and being are the same'.[3] It is likely that we become aware of our intellective activity when thought doubles back, and what is active in the life of the soul is reflected, like an image in the smooth, bright surface of a mirror held still. In such a case, in the presence of the mirror the reflection occurs; but even in the absence or unfavourable condition of the mirror, the object which would have been reflected is actually there. So with the soul: when the mirror in ourselves, in which images of thought and intellect appear, is held still, these are seen and recognised as if by perception, along with the prior knowledge that it is intellect and thought that are active. But when the mirror is shattered through disturbance of the body's harmony, the operation of thought and intellect casts no image, and intellection is unattended by a mental picture then. It follows that the operation of intellect may be accompanied by images, but is not itself an imaging.

One could cite many noble activities, theoretical or practical, that we perform when awake, which at the time do not engage our consciousness. The reader need not be conscious of reading, especially when reading with concentration, and in an act of courage there need be no consciousness of courage, or of acting in conformity with that virtue; and there are examples beyond number. Conscious acts of reflection are likely to blunt the very activities to which they are directed, activities which appear in their purity, more fully active and vital, only when unattended by reflection. And the sage, arrived at this state, enjoys a fuller life, not dissipated in sensation but concentrated in itself.

v) Happiness exists not in time, but in eternity

I 5.vii

Why shall we not say that the degree of happiness is determined by the time that it lasts? We should then treat happiness as divisible by the intervals of time, instead of making it indivisible by applying the measure of the present instant.

However, while there is nothing unreasonable in taking count of past time, which is no more than to count what once existed but is no more, like the dead; to reckon up past happiness as still existent, and as greater than present happiness, would be absurd. Being happy requires the existence of happiness, whereas time extending beyond the present is necessarily non-existent. Without exception, extension of time means the dispersal of a single present moment, and for this reason time is properly called 'the image of eternity',[4] since it tries to obliterate the abiding nature of eternity in its own dispersal. Therefore, if time robs eternity of its permanence and appropriates it, it destroys it; for though eternity may in some manner retain hold of it, it is destroyed by passing wholly into time.

If happiness depends on the good life, that life must obviously be located within the realm of Being, which is the pre-eminent Life, and must therefore be measured not by time, but by eternity; and there will be no more or less, or any magnitude, but only a 'this', unextended and timeless. We must not confuse Being with non-Being, nor time, even everlasting time, with eternity, and we must not extend the unextended; all must be taken together, if it may be grasped at all, not as a point of time but as the life of eternity, which is not an aggregate of time but outside all time, complete and self-contained.

vi) Matter is the cause of evil in the soul

I 8.iv

Corporeality, in so far as it partakes of matter, will be evil but not the primary evil. For bodies have a kind of unauthentic form and are bereft of life, and they destroy each other by their disorderly motion, which impedes the proper activity of the soul; they are in perpetual flux, and real Being eludes them. They are evil in the second degree, whereas Soul is not evil in itself, nor is every soul evil.

What is the evil soul? Plato talks of those who have 'enslaved the part of the soul in which evil naturally resides',[5] meaning the irrational aspect of the soul which is receptive of evil in the form of measurelessness, excess and deficiency; and these evils are the cause of licentiousness, cowardice and all other wickedness in the soul, involuntary affections that generate the false belief that the soul's likes and dislikes are the standard of good and evil.

What produces this wickedness, and how will it be related to the matter which is its source and cause? Firstly, this kind of soul is not apart from matter or by itself, and is therefore corrupted by the Measureless and wants form to give it order and bring it within measure; for the body in which it is merged contains matter. And then, if its reasoning faculty is impaired, its sight is obstructed by emotions and the darkening of matter, and by inclining to matter and fixing all its gaze not on Being, but on Becoming, whose principle is matter – matter so evil as to infect with its evil even what is not merged in it but only attends to it. Utterly devoid of good, a privation and sheer lack of good, matter assimilates to itself whatever makes any contact with it.

The perfect soul, directed towards Intellect, is always pure; it shuns matter, and all that is undetermined, without measure and evil it neither sees nor approaches, remaining in purity, wholly defined by Intellect. But the soul that abandons this state and deserts its true self, no longer perfect or primal but like an image of that other soul, becomes filled with the Indeterminate to the depth of its emptiness, and sees darkness; and now, in absorbing matter, it looks without seeing, as we are said to see darkness.

vii) The two kinds of Sin

IV 8.v

Every descent to a lower degree of existence is involuntary, but whatever descends by its own natural tendency is said to suffer the worse in retribution for its deeds. But when its sufferings and actions are determined by an eternal law of nature, and in its descent from the higher existence it meets the need of another in its approach to it, we would not be out of tune with the truth, or with our own nature, if we said that a god sent it down. It is to the origin of a process, however many stages intervene, that the ultimate outcome is referred.

Sin has two forms: the motive for the soul's descent, and the evil that it does when arrived in this world. The first is punished by the very experience of descent, the second, if the offence is slight, by brief immersion into other bodies, by judgement according to desert - the word 'judgement' signifying a divine decree; but all unbridled wickedness is condemned to severer retribution at the hands of avenging spirits.

Thus the soul, though of divine nature and a dweller in the world above, enters the body; it is a god of lower rank, and comes to this world by a voluntary leap, by its inherent power and from a desire to give order to what follows it. If it escapes quickly, it comes to no harm: it has acquired knowledge of evil and learned the nature of wickedness, and it has displayed its powers and brought forth works and actions which, had they remained latent in a bodiless existence, would have served no purpose, never reaching actuality; and the soul itself would have been ignorant of its powers if they had found no opening to reveal themselves.

Everywhere act reveals a potency wholly concealed, and virtually obliterated and non-existent if not brought to reality. As a consequence, the outer splendour prompts wonder at what lies within, and the Maker is judged by the fine finish of its works.

viii) The true meaning of Freedom

VI 8.i

What do we mean when we attribute to ourselves power over our actions, and why do we question this? My view is as follows.

Because we are driven by the chances and forces that oppose us, and the strong assaults of passion that grip the soul, supposing them all to be our masters, enslaved to them and borne along where they lead, we come to doubt if we are anything at all and if any action is within our power. Our assumption is that our action would be self-determined whenever we acted according to our will and with no opposition to our will, enslaved neither to chance nor to force nor to strong passion. In that case, our concept of self-determination will be action obedient to our will, and occurring or not according to the dictate of our will. All action is voluntary that is performed with knowledge and under no compulsion; and action that we are competent to perform will be within our power.

VI 8.iii

Action in obedience to fantasies caused by states of the body will not be ranked under the principle of self-determination; and men of depraved character, therefore, who act mostly in accordance with such fantasies, will be credited neither with power over their actions nor with voluntary action. We shall allow free-will only to those who act through intellect and are free from bodily affections, referring power over our actions to the highest principle, the activity of intellect. We shall count as truly free only the principles of action derived from intellect, and maintain that only desires roused by acts of intellect are not involuntary; and we shall attribute freedom to the gods, who live this life of intellect.

VI 8.iv

Yet it might be asked how action under the impulse of desire can be self-determined, when desire draws us beyond ourselves and implies a need; to desire is to be drawn, even if drawn towards the good. There must also be doubt about Intellect itself, if its freedom and self-determination are said to consist in acting according to its own nature; for what power does it have not so to act? Again, we must question whether it makes sense at all to ascribe self-determination to intelligible beings, who engage in no practical activity. Even for those who do so act, the compulsion is external, as their activity has a purpose. How, then, can there be freedom, when even these higher beings are slaves to their own nature?

On the other hand, if there is no compulsion to follow another, how can this be called slavery? And how can movement towards the good be termed compulsion, when the desire is voluntary if the good is recognised and pursued as good? Involuntary action is withdrawal from the good and submission to enforcement, a movement towards something other than one's own good; and slavery is to be powerless to pursue the good, and to be debarred from one's own good in servitude to some stronger master. This is why slavery is condemned, not as denying freedom to pursue evil, but as subjection to the good of another to the disregard of one's own good.

Further, talk of enslavement to one's nature implies a duality, the slave and the enslaver. But how can freedom be denied of a simple nature, a single actuality, admitting no distinction between the potential and actual? Action according to its nature cannot be predicated of it, as if its essence and activity were distinct; for to be and to act There are the same. Its activity is neither caused by nor in the power of another: it must therefore be free.

It may be that self-determination is an inappropriate term, inadequate to the reality; yet there is self-determination to the extent that intelligible being is not in another's power, and no other is master of its activity, or indeed of its being, as it is a principle. And though Intellect derives from a higher principle, this is not external to it, but it dwells within the Good; and if Intellect acts according to that Good, so much the more has it self-determination and freedom, which are sought for the sake of the Good. In acting according to the Good, therefore, it is self-determined, as possessing an inner impulse towards the Good and an aspiration tending to its own perfection, if directed to the Good.

ix) Death is a blessing for the soul
I 7.iii
If life is a good, does all that lives possess this good? No, for in the depraved character life is crippled, as in the eye of the dim-sighted, which fails in its task.

But if life, with its admixture of evil, is a good for us, surely death is an evil? Evil for whom? There must be a subject to suffer evil, but what no longer exists, or though existing, is devoid of life, is no more susceptible to evil than a stone. And if life and soul survive death, then there will still be good, and the more so now that soul acts purely according to its nature, unimpeded by body.

If it is absorbed into the World Soul, what evil can it suffer there? In sum, just as the gods enjoy good without taint of evil, so does the soul that maintains its purity; while if it lost its purity, not death but life would be its evil. Even if it suffer punishments in Hades, again it will be life, even there, that is the evil, because not life in its simple purity.

If life is a union of soul and body, and death their dissolution, then soul will welcome both - yet if life is good, how is death not an evil?

We answer that the good in life, where there is good, is due not to that union but to virtue's resistance to evil, and that death is the greater good. Life in a body must be accounted an evil in itself, and it is through virtue that the soul finds good - by not living according to the composite nature, but even now holding itself apart.

x) The sage's attitude to his body

I 4.xvi

Those who refuse to raise up the sage to this realm of Intellect, and drag him down to the world of chance, and fear him to be at risk from mere contingencies, have lost sight of the sage as we conceive him to be; they offer us a decent man, a blend of good and bad, and allot him the same blend of life - an unlikely possibility.

Even if such a one existed, he would not deserve to be called fulfilled; there is no greatness in him, whether the dignity of wisdom or the purity of goodness. The happy life cannot be the conjoint life of soul and body. Plato rightly insists that he who would attain wisdom and happiness must draw his good from that higher reality, fix his gaze on it, and be made like to that and live by that. This must be his only goal; all else he will treat as one changing his residence, not expecting any increase of happiness from his movements, but from regard for their effect on his exterior covering.

He will concede to his body what need demands, as far as he can, but he is distinct from it, with freedom to abandon it; and abandon it he will in nature's good time, by a decision of which he himself is master. Some of his conduct will contribute directly to his happiness, but not all his actions will have this goal in view, belonging not to himself but to the body appended to him; and he will care for this and bear with it while he can, like a musician for his lyre as long as he has use for it. When the lyre fails him, he will acquire another, or else dispense with the lyre and find a new role that has no need of a lyre; he will lay the lyre beside him unregarded, and sing without an instrument. Not that the instrument was idly given him at the beginning - he has often had use for it, until now.

REFERENCES

1. Plato, *Republic*, 590 a9, 588 c7.
2. Homer, *Iliad*, XXII 65.
3. Parmenides, *Diels* 83.
4. Plato, *Timaeus*, 37 d5.
5. Plato, *Phaedrus*, 256 b2-3.

VII
Purification and Virtue

Summary

i) We have seen (in V 1.ii) that a necessary preliminary to the purification and ascent of the human soul is to remind it of its kinship with the great Soul of the universe. Here, Plotinus raises a question forced on him by his own account of soul's relation to body. If the soul is not altered by affections, why should we strive to purify it? He answers that purification is not a change in the soul, but an awakening from the dream-images that the body transmits to its lower phase, so fixing its whole attention on higher reality.

The last sentence, which suggests that abstinence in diet should be part of the spiritual curriculum, contains a reference to the 'astral' body which was widely believed to house the soul. The belief influenced Christian teaching concerning the resurrection of the body, but was itself condemned by the Church.

ii) The Gnostic teaching, that salvation comes by way of privileged knowledge alone, is destructive of morality. The disciplined practice of the virtues is a necessary part of the way of purification.

Historically, it is a fact that some Gnostic sects adopted an antinomian stance and abandoned moral restraint, particularly in sexual behaviour.

iii) The ascent to the vision of the Good is not for everyone, but only those with a predisposition to appreciate disembodied form and beauty, and an aptitude for moral and aesthetic education and the formal disciplines of mathematics and dialectic.

The curriculum is Platonic, recalling especially the *Republic* and the *Symposium*.

iv) If the practice of moral virtue is necessary to the purification of the soul, it must be shown how the virtues contribute to the attainment of 'likeness to god'.

Aristotle's distinction between intellectual virtues and moral virtues is adapted by Plotinus to a theory of higher and lower - or social - virtues; at each level he discusses the four 'cardinal' virtues traditional in Greek thought - justice, moderation, courage and prudence.

The Platonist Albinus had argued that virtue cannot produce likeness to a deity who transcends virtue. Plotinus' reply is ingenious.

v) Perfection of virtue raises the soul to the status of a god, restored to the intelligible world of its origin. This extract explains the character of the virtues in the sage.

i) The meaning of Purification and separation in the soul
III 6.v

Why should we seek, by the influence of philosophy, to make the soul immune to affections, if it has always been impassive?

When the so-called affective part of the soul is attacked by a mental representation producing a resultant reaction, or disturbance, and the image of the expected evil is coupled with the disturbance, we call this experience an affection. Reason deems it right to eliminate all such experience and deny it to the soul, as destructive of soul's health; and if the image in the soul, the cause of the affection, is removed, then soul will be immune. Similarly, one might dispel dream-images by waking the soul from its fantasies, and say that the soul had produced the affections, meaning that the images, seen as external realities, were the affections of the soul.

But what could be meant by the 'purification' of a soul that has never been defiled, and by its 'separation'[1] from the body? Purification would be to leave it alone and isolated, concerned with nothing outside itself and holding no alien impressions - whatever the character of such impressions or affections, as we have said - so as to entertain no images nor build them into affections. And surely the opposite tendency, the ascent from the lower to the higher reality, is the purification and separation of a soul divorcing itself from the body and disowning it? It is like a light emerging from the mists - yet untouched even when obscured. And the purification of the affective part is its awakening from frivolous images and their banishment from its sight, and its separation a reluctance to decline, a freedom from earthly imaginings. Separation might also mean the abolition of everything from which it distances itself, when the spiritual body in which it rests is not turbid from gluttony and a surfeit of unclean flesh, but a slender form, fit to convey it in tranquillity.

ii) The Gnostic doctrine destroys moral responsibility
II 9.xv

One matter which we must on no account overlook is the effect of these doctrines on the souls of those who receive them, and are persuaded to despise the world and everything in it.

There are two schools of thought on the attainment of the end of life, one of which proposes bodily pleasure as the end, while the other declares for goodness and virtue, the desire for which, it holds, derives from God and leads back to God, as may be studied elsewhere. Epicurus, who denies Providence, urges the pursuit of pleasure and its enjoyment, as all that is left to us; but the Gnostic teaching, with even greater abandon, impugns the Lord of Providence and Providence itself, discredits all human laws and time-honoured virtue, and scoffs at moderation, that nothing noble should be seen on earth; it eliminates self-discipline and the righteousness, innate in men's characters, that is perfected by reason and training. In short, whatever makes for human excellence, it destroys. They are left with pleasure, self-interest that excludes their fellow men, and mere fulfilment of need – except where character proves superior to their teachings; nothing here has value for them, and their good lies elsewhere, beyond this present life.

And yet, possessed of secret knowledge, they should begin the quest here, first setting right their conduct as befits visitors from the Divine, of a nature that appreciates nobility and scorns bodily pleasure; for those with no part in virtue will feel no spur to rise.

They stand convicted also by their lack of teaching on virtue, their utter failure to discuss its nature and its separate elements, their neglect of the many valuable theories in the literature of the past; they are silent on the causes that produce virtue and the means of its attainment, on the tendance and purification of the soul. For to say 'Look to God' is no help, without instructions on how to look rightly. A man might say, 'What prevents me from looking without sacrifice of pleasure, remaining the slave of impulse and, while remembering the name "God", being possessed by every passion and making no effort to banish them?'

It is, on the contrary, virtue, when implanted in the soul in conjunction with wisdom, that advances to the good and shows us God; but without true virtue, 'God' is no more than a name.

iii) The musician, the lover and the philosopher

I 3.i

What art or method or discipline will take us to our journey's end? That our destination is the Good, or First Principle, we may take to be agreed and demonstrated at length; moreover, the demonstrations have themselves served to lead us on the upward path.

And he who shall follow this path, what kind of man must he be? Surely one who has seen all or 'most of the world of Being', as Plato says, 'and in the first birth been conceived as a man destined to be a philosopher, a musician or a lover'.[2] To make the ascent is inherent in the philosophic nature, while the musician and the lover need a guide. What, then, is the way? Is it one and the same for them all, or is there a separate way for each?

For everyone the journey has two stages, the ascent and what follows the ascent. The first leads from the world below, while the second is for those already arrived in the Intelligible, who have gained a footing there but must travel till they reach the furthest limit of that realm, 'the end of the journey',[3] when they stand upon the summit of intelligible Being. But let that wait; we must first try to describe the ascent.

Firstly, we must distinguish these men, and begin by describing the character of the musician. We must suppose him to be quickly moved and excited by beauty, and though somewhat insensitive to the power of absolute Beauty, yet readily affected on encountering its images; and just as the timid react to noises, so is he prompt to react to sounds and the beauty conveyed in them, shunning all discordance and disunity in song and rhythm, and longing for good measure and form. He must be led on, therefore, beyond these perceptible sounds, rhythms and patterns, to abstract the material from the forms in which proportions and principles of order reside; he must be guided to the Beauty that illumines them, and taught that the origin of his passion was the harmony of the Intelligible, and the beauty in it, and not one particular beauty, but universal Beauty. And the lessons of philosophy must be implanted in him, to establish a firm faith in the truths that he unwittingly possesses. What these lessons are will be shown later.

I 3.ii

The musician may be transformed into the lover, and either be content so or pass beyond.

The lover has a kind of recollection of Beauty, but is parted from it and cannot comprehend it; he is overwhelmed by visible beauties as the present focus of his passion. He must be taught not to find rapture in the worship of a single body, but be guided by reason to see the same Beauty in all embodied form, and be brought to understand its incorporeal nature and higher origin, and its truer manifestation in the immaterial. He should be shown the beauty in customs and laws, as a first lesson in disembodied loveliness, and learn to see the beauty in arts, sciences and virtues. Next, these forms of beauty must be brought under one principle, and their source explained. From virtues he must now ascend to Intellect, or Being itself; and once there, must tread the higher path.

I 3.iii

The philosopher, prepared for the ascent by his very character, and 'winged' already, in no need of separation, like those others, is self-impelled towards the upward path, and in his uncertainty wants only a guide. He must be shown the way and given release, a willing traveller and in temperament already liberated. He must learn mathematics, to develop abstract thought and a firm faith in incorporeal reality, and this he will easily assimilate, as a lover of learning. Virtuous by nature, he must be guided to the perfection of his virtues; and after mathematics, he must be taught dialectical argument and be made a master of Dialectic.

iv) Likeness to God is attained through Virtue

I 2.i

Since evil belongs to this world, and 'haunts this region, of necessity', and the soul desires to escape from evil, 'we must escape from here'. What is the way of escape? 'Attaining likeness to God', in Plato's words; and this is 'to become just and holy under the guidance of wisdom',[4] and wholly in virtue. If, therefore, likeness is attained by virtue, does God possess virtue? And what God will this be?

Does the Intelligible possess virtue? It defies reason that the so-called social virtues should be found there – prudence that employs the reasoning faculty, courage that relates to the emotions, moderation that consists in harmonious agreement between desire and reason, and justice, which is the exercise of each of these 'about its own business, in respect of governing or obeying.'[5] So is likeness not attained by the social virtues, but by those greater virtues that bear the same names? And if by other virtues, are the social virtues an irrelevance?

It would be unreasonable to allow no part to these, but only to the greater virtues, in the attainment of likeness to the Divine; at any rate, hallowed tradition gives the name of godlike to men of social virtue, and we must say that they attained to likeness in some manner. It is possible to possess virtues on both levels, though not the same virtues. So if it is agreed that likeness can be attained, though not through the same virtues, and that different virtues are appropriate to corporeal beings, there is nothing to prevent our attaining likeness, by our own virtues, to one that transcends virtue, if the likeness is not identity of virtue.

How can this be? Consider: if something is heated by the presence of heat, must the source of the heat itself be heated? And if something is hot by the presence of fire, must the fire itself be heated by the presence of fire? To the first example it might be objected that there is heat in fire as its inherent property, and if the analogy were pursued it could be argued that, whereas virtue is extraneous to the soul, it is inherent in the source from where the soul derives it by imitation. And to the example of fire, it may be claimed that this makes the Principle identical with virtue, whereas we hold it to be greater than virtue.

This objection would stand if that in which soul participates were identical with the Ideal; but in fact, the two are distinct. The house perceived by the senses is not identical with the intelligible house, though made in its likeness; the perceptible house exhibits order and design, but in that higher principle that gives it form, there is neither order nor design nor proportion. If, therefore, we similarly derive design, order and harmony from the Intelligible, and these constitute virtue in this world, while intelligible beings have no need of harmony, design or order, then they will have no need of virtue either, and we nonetheless attain likeness to them by the presence of virtue.

This argument is sufficient to show that our attaining likeness by virtue does not entail the presence of virtue in the Intelligible; but we must not rely on force of argument, but make our case persuasive.

I 2.ii

First, we must take the virtues by which we claim that likeness is attained, to discover the identical constituent which is virtue when possessed by us as a copy, but in the Intelligible not virtue, but its archetype. We must make it clear that likeness is twofold: there is the likeness that requires an identical element in the things that are alike, which is found when their likeness derives from a common exemplar; but when two things are alike but one has primacy, not being convertible to the other or describable as similar, then we must interpret likeness in a different sense, and expect not the same form in both, but diversity of form corresponding to the different mode of likeness.

What, then, is virtue, both in general and in the particular? Discussion of particular virtues will make for a clearer account, as this will readily reveal the common element by which they are all virtues.

The social virtues, mentioned above, are principles of order and ennoblement which set limit and measure to our desires, confine all our affections within bounds, and abolish false judgements; this they achieve by a general betterment and regulation, by ousting the unlimited and indeterminate in favour of the measured, by their own defined character. In that they are measures informing the matter of the soul, they resemble measure in the realm of Being and carry a trace of intelligible perfection. The utterly measureless is matter, in which there is no likeness to the divine; but to the extent that it shares in form, it becomes like that One which is without form. Participation is greater with proximity, and Soul, closer and more akin than body, participates more fully, revealed as a god, and creating the delusion that Soul comprises all divinity.

It is thus that men of social virtue attain likeness to God.

I 2.iii

But Plato suggests that another mode of likeness belongs to the greater virtues, and of this we must now speak. The discussion will clarify the essence of both social virtue and the greater kind, and the distinction between them.

In describing 'likeness' as 'escape to God' from the things of this world, and in referring not simply to 'virtues' in the social context, but adding the qualification 'social' virtues, while elsewhere using the term 'purifications'[6] for all virtues, Plato evidently posits two kinds of virtue and denies that likeness is attained merely at the social level. In what sense, then, are these other virtues called 'purifications', and how is it that likeness is most fully attained by purification?

As the soul is evil by intermixture with the body, sharing the body's affections and thinking all its thoughts, it will be good and possessed of virtue by rejecting the body's judgements, and acting alone – which is the exercise of intellect and wisdom; by resisting the body's affections – which is moderation; by having no fear of being parted from the body – which is courage; and by unreserved obedience to reason and intellect – and this is justice. Such a state of the soul, intellective and unaffected by passion, may without error be called likeness to God; for the Divine, too, is pure, and its activity the perfect exemplar of its image, wisdom.

Why, then, is the Divine not so disposed? It has no states, for they belong to soul. And intellection takes different forms in soul and in the Intelligible, while in the One there is no thought at all. Again: is 'intellection', then, ambiguous? Not at all, intellection may be primal or derivative. As the spoken word echoes the thought in the soul, so the thought in the soul has its source in another; and the soul's thought is fragmented in utterance, as it fragmented that prior thought that it interprets. Virtue belongs to soul; not to Intellect, nor to the Transcendent.

v) The nature of the virtues in the purified soul

I 2.v

We must state how far the purification extends, to make it clear what likeness is attained and with what god we become identified. This is equivalent to asking how far the process eliminates passion and desire and all other affections, including pain and its kindred, and how far separation from the body is possible.

The soul withdraws from the body, as if to its own place: holding itself entirely indifferent to it, it recognises only such pleasures as are necessary and bring healing and relief of labour, lest its work be impeded, and it dispels pains, or where it cannot, bears them easily and reduces them by standing apart from the body's suffering. Passion it rejects entirely, when it can, and never surrenders to its influence, treating all involuntary feeling as alien and ineffective intrusion. Fear is unknown to it, beyond that involuntary trace, except to admonish: for there is nothing for it to fear. What of desire? Evidently it will desire no evil object, nor will it crave indulgence in food, drink or sexual pleasure; these will be desired as natural needs, unaccompanied by involuntary impulse, or at least by no more than idle fantasies.

Purified of all such affections, soul will desire further to cleanse the irrational nature, and so fortify it against all assaults, and to reduce their effect and bring swift release by its own presence; just as the neighbour of a sage might profit from his company, either by taking on his virtues or, out of shame, never daring by his acts to incur the good man's displeasure. There will be no conflict: the presence of reason will suffice to shame the lower nature, which will view its own stirrings with disgust, and censure its own weakness for not keeping calm in the presence of its lord.

I 2.vi

Yet while there is no sin in this, but only good conduct for a man, our concern is not merely to be sinless, but to be god. While any trace of the involuntary survives, such a man would be god and demi-god, a twofold nature, or god accompanied by one of different quality; but where no trace remains, he will be purely god, a god among those who follow the First. The man is himself the god who descended, and his true nature is on high, if he will become his former self; and to the best of his divine power he will raise his partner in this world to his own likeness, rendering it immune to affections and teaching it to forbear from any action condemned by its lord.

What form does each virtue take in a man so restored? Wisdom and prudence consist in the contemplation of that content of Intellect with which intellect has immediate contact. Each has two modes, one in intellect, one in soul; and that in soul is virtue, but that in intellect not virtue. What then? In the higher realm, the self's act and essence; descended here below, virtue, residing in another. The ideal form – of justice, for example – is not virtue, but as it were an exemplar, and virtue is its image in the soul. Virtue has its possessor, but the Ideal belongs to none but itself.

Justice is defined as each performing its proper function, but this does not always entail plurality. There is the justice in plurality, where the elements are multiple, and proper functioning as such, even in a unity. True justice in its ideal form is a relation of a unity to itself, with no diversity of parts.

In the soul, therefore, justice – in its higher form – is its activity directed to intellect; moderation, its turning inward to intellect; and courage, its indifference to affections, in the likeness of that impassive nature to which it directs its gaze, an indifference acquired by virtue to shield it from the turbulence of its baser companion.

REFERENCES

1. Plato, *Phaedo*, 67 c5–6.
2. Plato, *Phaedrus*, 248 d1–4.
3. Plato, *Republic*, 532 e3.
4. Plato, *Theaetetus*, 176 a–b.
5. Plato, *Republic*, 434 c8, 443 b2.
6. Plato, *Phaedo*, 82 a11, 69 c1.

VIII
Beauty

Summary

i) The view that beauty is, or is dependent on, proportion was a commonplace of Greek philosophy. Plotinus seeks to refute it, and to identify beauty with the invisible and intelligible Form (not itself a thing of proportion) which stands as archetype to the work of art or nature.

His statement that the parts of a beautiful whole must themselves be beautiful conflicts with his use of aesthetic analogies in discussing the place of evil in the world.

ii) In the *Republic* (Book X) Plato disparages works of art as mere copies of material objects which are themselves copies of intelligible forms, and so far removed from reality. Plotinus in this chapter presents the more positive view that the mind of the artist has direct access to ideal forms.

iii) The soul recognises beauty in the sensible world by reference to the higher, intelligible world to which it has access.

iv) The soul may ascend from embodied beauty to the appreciation of abstract beauty, as exemplified by the virtues. Just as ugliness in the soul is caused by immersion in the body, so beauty in the soul is its purification by virtue.

v) The Good is the transcendent source of the ideal Beauty of Intellect, which in its turn informs Soul and the beauty in the world of sense. The soul purified by virtue attains likeness to God by raising itself to the realm of pure Being.

vi) The supreme attainment of the soul is the vision of the Good, the transcendent cause of Beauty, for which 'a different way of seeing' is needed, acquired by the patient process of inner purification.

Whereas Plato identifies the Good with Beauty, Plotinus is usually careful to preserve the transcendence of the infinite Good over the perfect Beauty of the world of Being. The Good is 'Beauty above Beauty'.

vii) Even the highest Beauty may be a distraction to the soul in its ascent to the Good. The passions aroused by Beauty are contrasted with the stillness of mystical union.

i) Refutation of the theory that beauty is good proportion

I 6.1

Almost everyone states that the beauty recognised by the eye arises from good proportion in the parts, in their relation to each other and to the whole, enhanced by the effect of colour; and that visual beauty, and indeed beauty in general, consists of good proportion and measure. On this view, it necessarily follows that no simple object, but only what is composite, can be beautiful; and that it will be the whole that has beauty, while the separate parts have no beauty in themselves, but only contribute to the beauty of the whole.

However, the beauty of the whole entails beauty in the parts, and is quite incompatible with ugliness in the detail; beauty must pervade every part. And again, the theory implies that beautiful colours, like the sunlight, which have no parts and therefore no beauty dependent on proportion, must be excluded from the realm of the beautiful. And how, on this account, can gold be beautiful? And what gives beauty to lightning in the night sky, and to the stars? Consider sounds also: the same ban will be placed on single sounds, and yet often in a beautiful composition there is beauty in each separate sound. And when the same face sometimes appears beautiful, but sometimes not, though the proportions remain constant, must it not follow that beauty is more than good proportion, that the beauty in proportion derives from some further principle? Pass on again to the beauty in customs and discourse: will this also be attributed to good proportion? In what sense could beautiful customs, or laws, or theoretical knowledge be said to possess symmetry? How can theories be symmetrical with each other? If concordance is meant, there can be agreement and concordance in ugliness: the propositions that righteousness is noble simplemindedness, and that self-discipline is folly, are concordant and harmonious, in full agreement the one with the other. Every virtue, too, is a beauty of the soul, and a more real beauty than those others – but where is the symmetry? It cannot be the symmetry of magnitude or numbers, and though the soul is complex, by what principle could its faculties and thought be synthesised and blended? And what would be the beauty of pure Intellect in isolation?

I 6.ii

So let us begin again, and explain first of all the nature of embodied beauty. It is something that is perceived even at the first glance, and the soul speaks of it as if familiar with it, recognises and welcomes it and, in a way, comes into union with it; whereas on encountering ugliness it shrinks back, disowns it and recoils from it, out of harmony and estranged. We maintain that, by its special nature and derivation from that higher reality in the scale of Being, the soul thrills with delight whenever it sees its kin or a trace of its kin, and takes it to itself, awakening the memory of its own origin and kindred.

What resemblance exists, then, between earthly and heavenly beauty? Let us grant the resemblance; but what links the two orders of beauty? Participation in ideal Form, we maintain, is the source of earthly beauty. For all that is shapeless, though of a nature to admit shape and form, is ugly and beyond the reach of divine Reason, by its very want of rational Form; and this is absolute ugliness. Ugly also is what is not mastered by pattern and formative Reason, because its matter has not yielded entirely to the imprint of Form. The form, on its approach, orders what is to emerge from multiplicity into a unified composition, achieves a single realisation, and makes it one by its inner harmony; for as the form is a unity itself, what is shaped by it must be a unity within the limits imposed by multiplicity. Upon this new-formed unity Beauty sits enthroned, giving itself both to parts and whole; and when it lights upon a unity consisting of like parts, it gives the same gift to the whole. So, for example, there is the beauty that art gives to a house with all its parts, and the beauty that nature gives to a single stone. This, then, is how embodied beauty comes to be, through communion with informing Reason that descends from divine Being.

ii) Ideal Beauty in Art

V 8.i

Since we maintain that one who has enjoyed contemplation of the intelligible world and apprehended the beauty of true Intellect will be able also to conceive of its Father, who is beyond Intellect, let us try to see and explain to ourselves, as far as such matters can be put into words, how one might contemplate the beauty of Intellect and of that higher world.

Let us imagine, if you will, two large stones lying side by side, one formless and untouched by art, the other already mastered by art and transformed into the statue of a divinity, such as a Grace or Muse, or else of a human being, and not just of any human being, but one on which art has lavished every kind of beauty. The stone on which art has bestowed beauty of form will appear beautiful not because it is a stone – for in that case the other would be equally beautiful, but because of the form imparted to it by art.

Now this form was not in the material, but in the craftsman who conceived the statue even before it entered the stone; and it was in him not inasmuch as he had eyes or hands, but by virtue of his artistry. So this Beauty belonged to art, an ideal and far superior Beauty; for it was not the original Beauty in art that entered the stone, but a lesser, derivative beauty, and even this did not keep its purity or perfect its intention in the stone, but only so far as the stone yielded to art.

If art creates an image of itself and its own, and makes its work beautiful by a principle that gives form to it, it is itself beautiful in a higher and truer sense, since it possesses the Beauty of art which surpasses any beauty in the external object. In proportion as form is extended on entering into matter, it becomes weaker than what remains in unity. Everything in being extended suffers some loss – strength becomes less strong, heat less hot, any power less potent, beauty less beautiful. The creator must always be intrinsically superior to its creation: it is music, not an unmusical source, that makes a musician, and the art in the world of sense derives from that in the higher world. If anyone despises the arts because they create by imitating nature, we must first insist that the works of nature are themselves imitations; and further, we must recognise that the arts do not simply imitate what meets the eye, but go beyond to the principles that inform nature. They also contribute much of themselves; they have beauty in their possession and supply what may be lacking. Pheidias, for example, created his Zeus not after any perceptible model, but from an apprehension of what Zeus would be like if he wished to appear to our sight.

iii) The recognition of embodied beauty

I 6.iii

Soul recognises beauty by a faculty receptive to it, one with special authority to judge its own, when the rest of soul supports its judgement; or perhaps soul itself pronounces, making comparison with the Form within itself and using this for its judgement as a canon of accuracy.

How can there be accord between the material and the immaterial that precedes it? How can the architect pronounce the house before him to be beautiful on comparing it to the form of house within him? Surely the external object, apart from the stones, is the inner form distributed in the mass of external matter, indivisible in reality but under the appearance of multiplicity. So when sense-perception sees embodied form that has bound and mastered the shapeless matter that opposes it, and one shape riding pre-eminent upon all other shapes, it gathers together the fragmented vision, and takes it up and brings it within, now undivided, and presents it to the principle in soul, as something concordant, conformable and dear to it; just as a good man delights to see a trace of virtue in a youth concordant with his own inner ideal.

So much for the beauties of sense, images and shadows escaped into matter, that adorn and excite when they appear.

iv) The beauties of the purified soul
I 6.iv

But there are transcendent beauties, beyond the reach of perception, which soul without organs of sense sees and proclaims; and to contemplate these we must leave sense below, and ascend. Just as the beauties of sense cannot be told by those who have not seen them or grasped their beauty - people born blind for example, in the same way the beauty of customs eludes description by those unappreciative of them, and of learning and all such activities; nor can the splendour of virtue be told by those who have not even imagined how fair is the face of justice and moderation - and 'neither the evening nor the morning star is as fair'.[1]

But there must be those who see with the faculty with which soul beholds such beauties, and they will rejoice at the sight with a shock and a thrill far greater than that corporeal beauty could stir; for they now grasp true beauties. These are the feelings that any beauty must arouse: wonder, an awe-struck delight, and longing and love and a quivering of pleasure. These feelings may be excited by unseen beauties, and virtually all souls experience them, but especially those with a deeper love for unseen reality;

just as all see the beauty in bodies but not all are stung as sharply, and those who feel the sharpest pang are called lovers.

I 6.v

But what is it that arouses this passion? Not shape, not colour, not anything extended, but Soul. Soul itself has no colour, and the moral wisdom and all the splendour of the virtues that it owns have no colour; yet it is the source of that passion, whenever you see in yourself, or in another, magnanimity, a righteous character, moderation and purity, grim-visaged courage, gravity and modesty, all contained in an untroubled, calm and tranquil disposition – and over all the godlike light of Intellect.

We reverence and love these virtues, but why do we call them beautiful? They exist and appear to us, and he who sees them cannot deny that they have real Being. In what sense, real Being? Of course, beauty – but we must still explain by what character they make the soul beautiful. What is this splendour as of light that plays upon all the virtues?

Shall we take the contrary, the ugliness in soul, for comparison? Perhaps our search will be advanced if we learn the nature of ugliness and why it appears.

Let us suppose, then, an ugly soul, dissolute and unrighteous, teeming with lusts and racked with strife, with the fear of the coward and the jealousies of the mean-minded, its limited thought confined to base and mortal objects, perverted utterly, a lover of unclean pleasures, and living a life of bodily sensation, delighting in its ugliness. Shall we not say that all this ugliness that it sees as beauty is some alien accretion, violating and polluting it; and that, infected with all manner of evil, its life and perception sullied, it lives a frail and death-ridden life, no longer seeing what soul should see, no longer left at peace in itself, but for ever drawn to the external, the lower, the dark? An impure soul, without doubt, lured in every direction by the objects of sense, heavily influenced by bodily desire, sunk deep in matter and absorbing matter, its commerce with evil has disfigured its true form.

If a man sinks into mud or filth he no longer displays his former beauty, and the mud or filth smeared upon him is all that is seen. His ugliness is the accretion of alien matter, and his task, to recover his grace, is to cleanse and purify himself so as to be as he was before.

We should be right, therefore, to say that ugliness in the soul is its infection and pollution by descent towards body and matter. The ugly soul is not, like gold, pure and unadulterated, but filled with the dross of earth; remove this, and the gold remains and is beautiful, stripped of its accretions, in all its purity. In the same way the soul, when secluded from the lusts of the body, with which it was too intimate, when given release and purged of all passions aroused by embodiment, remains by itself, all alien deformity put off.

v) Beauty in the soul is to escape from body into Intellect

I 6.vi

It was said by Plato that moderation, courage and every virtue, and even wisdom itself, is a purification. This is the truth of those symbolic words of the mystery rites, that the man unpurified will lie in filth even in Hades; for filth is congenial to the impure by the evil in it, as it delights pigs, unclean in body. What else could true moderation be but to avoid association with bodily pleasures, and to shun them as impure affections of a thing impure? Courage is fearlessness in the face of death, and death is the separation of soul from body; and he does not fear this, whose wish is to be alone. Magnanimity is disdain for the things of this world, and wisdom is thought which turns from the world below and leads the soul to the higher reality. So the soul when purified becomes pure form and formative power, all disembodied and intellective, and wholly within the Divine, which is the fount of Beauty and all its kin. In ascending to intellect, soul's beauty is heightened. Intellect and its issue are its own proper beauty, because only as intellect is it perfectly soul. It is therefore right to say that for the soul to become good and beautiful is to be made like to God; for he is the source of Beauty and all else that belongs to Being.

Or rather, Being is absolute Beauty, and the contrary principle is Ugliness, the primal evil. For the One, therefore, good and beautiful, or the Good and absolute Beauty, are the same. So the same method of search leads to Goodness and Beauty and to Ugliness and Evil. At the head must be set absolute Beauty, which is also the Good; from this derives Intellect, which is the Beautiful; and by Intellect Soul is made beautiful. All lower existents have beauty by the informing power of Soul - actions and customs, for example, and beautiful bodies. For Soul is a thing divine, like a portion of Beauty, and makes beautiful everything it grasps and controls, to the limit of their receptiveness.

vi) The way of ascent to the vision of the supreme Beauty
I 6.vii

We must therefore ascend again to the Good, for which every soul yearns. Whoever has seen it knows what I mean in calling it beautiful. Even the desire for this is to be desired as a good; and the attainment of it is for those who make the ascent and turn to it, and strip off the coverings we have put on in our descent, just as those who ascend to the inner sanctuary of the temples must first be purified and put off their former garments and enter naked; until, after passing on the ascent all that is alien to God, each one sees in his own solitude the solitary Good, unalloyed, simple and pure, from which all things depend, and towards which all things look and exist and live and think, as the cause of Life and Mind and Being.

Should anyone see this, what pangs of love would he feel, what yearnings to be blest with it, what a shock of delight? He who has not seen may yearn for it as good; but he who has seen will marvel at its beauty, and be filled with wonder and delight and a sense of awe that brings no hurt; his love will be true love and his passion keen, and he will despise all other loves and disdain all that he once thought beautiful. Such also is the feeling of those who, after encountering gods or spirits in visible form, no longer take the same pleasure in the beauty of other bodies. What then shall we think of one who should contemplate absolute Beauty in its essential purity, not housed in flesh or body, not in earth nor in heaven, that it may keep its purity? For these are all extraneous, alloys, not primal but descended from that First. If one should see that Good, which provides for all but in self-contentment takes nothing for itself, what further beauty would one need, but to continue in its contemplation and find delight to be made like to it? For this is Beauty supreme and pre-eminent, which fashions its lovers in beauty and makes them lovable. Here it is that souls face their greatest and ultimate challenge, and for this is all their labour, not to be excluded from the supreme vision; for blessed is the man who has beheld the blessed sight, but he who fails has failed utterly.

To fail is not the want of beauty in colours or bodies, nor the want of power, offices or kingship, but the want of this Beauty only; and for this a man should forego kingship and dominion over all the earth and sea and sky, if by foresaking these he may turn to face that Beauty and behold it.

I 6.viii

What then is the way, and what the means? How may we behold a mysterious Beauty that stays within the temple sanctuary, never emerging to uninitiated eyes? He who has the strength must follow the path within, forsaking the sights outside and turning his back on the material splendours that he knew before. When he sees embodied beauties he must not pursue them, but know them for images, traces and shadows, and take flight to the Reality that they represent. A myth tells of one wishing to grasp a fair reflection playing on the water, who sank beneath the stream and disappeared; which I believe to symbolise the man who runs to seize an image as if it were reality. For in the same way he who clings to material beauties and will not reject them will plunge, not in body but in soul, down to the dark depths loathed by the mind, and will remain blind in Hades, consorting with shadows there as here.

'Then let us take flight to our dear native land'[2] - this would be wiser counsel. So what shall be our course, and how shall we sail? We shall put out to sea as Odysseus did, to escape the witch Circe or Calypso - not content to stay, for all the sights that delighted his eyes and the beauty that charmed his senses; for there is hidden meaning, I believe, in Homer's tale. For us, our native land from where we came, and our Father, are There above.

What then should be our voyage and our flight? We cannot travel there on foot, for our feet never carry us but from land to land; nor should you prepare a carriage or a ship. No, you must set all such things aside and refuse to look. Close your eyes and wake to life a different way of seeing, which all possess but few employ.

I 6.ix

And what does that inner sight behold? At its first awakening it cannot bear the brightness of the vision. So the soul itself must be trained, first to behold beautiful customs, then works of beauty - not those produced by the arts, but by the virtue of men of good repute; and next, observe the souls of those who fashion these beauties.

How might you see the beauty in a virtuous soul? Retire into yourself, and look; and if you cannot yet see beauty in yourself, learn from the sculptor giving beauty to his statue: he cuts away here and polishes there, smoothing and cleaning, till his statue wears a beautiful face. You, similarly, must cut away excesses, straighten what is crooked, lighten what is dark and make it bright, and never cease from 'working on your statue' till the godlike glory of virtue shines out on you, till you see 'righteousness firmly established on its holy pedestal'.[3]

If you have achieved this and have seen this vision, and in purity become at one with yourself, with nothing to impede or defile this inner unity, wholly yourself, true light alone; not confined within measure or reduced within limits of shape, but yet not extended to infinite magnitude - measureless everywhere, as greater than all measure and more than all quantity: if you see that you have grown to this, then you have become sight itself. Take heart now; you have made the ascent and no longer need a guide. Gaze, and see: this eye alone can behold the great Beauty.

vii) The intelligible Beauty distinguished from the Good

V 5.xi

The objects that are taken to be prime instances of reality are unreal in the extreme, and extension is a diminution. But the First is the source of Reality and in authority over Being. You must therefore reverse your way of thinking, or be left deprived of God, like people at the festivals who gorge themselves in their gluttony with foods forbidden to those who would approach the gods; they suppose them to be more real than the vision of the god in whose honour the feast is held, and take no part in the rites within. Similarly, in these inward rites of ours, the god's invisibility makes his existence doubted by those who only judge reality by what they see in the flesh. It is as if they slept all their life and took their dreams on trust to be reality; and if they were woken, they would distrust the evidence of their open eyes and fall asleep again.

V 5.xii

Everything must be perceived by its appropriate faculty, some things by sight, others by hearing, and so on. And we can be sure that intellect has its own objects, and must not confuse intellection with hearing or sight, which would be like delegating vision to the ears, or denying the existence of sounds because they are invisible. We must bear in mind that some have forgotten what has been their longing and their goal from the beginning. For all things reach out to him and aspire to him by a compulsion of nature, as if divining that without him they cannot exist. The apprehension of Beauty, and the wonder and waking of love for it, belong to those who already know it, in a way, and are awake, whereas the Good, long present object of innate desire, is present even to those who sleep, and a sight of it causes no shock, as it is always within them, needing no recall, though while they sleep its presence is unseen. The love of Beauty, when it appears, causes pain, because those who see it must pursue. That this love is secondary, only felt by the attentive, declares Beauty itself to be secondary; while the more primitive and unconscious desire is witness that the Good has the primacy and priority over it.

All consider the Good to be sufficient for them, when they have attained it: they have reached their goal. But not all have seen Beauty, and when it appears they judge it beautiful for itself, and not for them, like the beauty in this world, which belongs to its possessor. And a semblance of Beauty suffices, without the reality; but no one rests content with a mere seeming Good. All have the First as their supreme desire, but they quarrel jealously with Beauty as something of secondary rank like themselves. In just such a way might one of minor rank at court covet equal status with the king's first minister, on the ground of common dependence, not realising that, for all he owes to the king, the other holds the higher rank. The cause of the error is that both share a common source and the Monarch rules them both; and similarly in that higher reality, the Good itself has no need of Beauty, but Beauty needs the Good.

The Good is gentle, kindly and tender, and present to us at our will; but Beauty astounds and shocks and brings pain with its pleasure. Again, it even lures the unknowing away from the Good, as the beloved lures a child from its father; for Beauty is younger. The Good is older, not in time but in reality, and has the prior power; for it has all power; while the subordinate possesses not all power but a secondary power, in his bestowal and under his lordship.

The Good has no need of his creatures, and is careless of his whole creation; he required nothing from it, and is the same as before he brought it into being. He would have been unconcerned, had it not come to be; and if another world might have derived from him, he would not have grudged it existence. As it is, nothing more can exist; for when the universe of things exists, there is nothing uncreated.

He was not that universe, or would have been contingent on it; but transcending the universe, he had power to create it and let it be, while himself remaining above it.

REFERENCES

1. Aristotle, *Nicomachean Ethics*, 1129b, 28–9.
2. Homer, *Iliad*, II 140.
3. Plato, *Phaedrus*, 252d, 254b.

IX
Intellectual Contemplation

Summary

i) Our attention fixed on our higher soul, we become aware of our divine nature. Each one of us is an 'intelligible universe' in that, at the level of intellect, we contain the whole of intelligible Being.

'The sciences latent within' refers to Dialectic, the study of pure Being, which in this extract means the direct intuition of intelligible reality by the risen soul. Plotinus also uses the term 'Dialectic' to refer to the theoretical discipline which is a preliminary to contemplation.

ii) A mental exercise to induce the vision of the divine Intellect in its manifold unity.

The procession of the gods is borrowed from Plato's *Phaedrus* (246e, ff.). Plotinus takes Uranos, Kronos and Zeus to symbolise his three hypostases, Zeus representing Soul.

The soul in this extract transcends detached contemplation and attains perfect integration with the Intelligible, becoming no longer a spectator but the vision itself. The comparison with drunkenness and divine possession shows this to be a state intermediate between intellectual contemplation and contact with the One, a mystical experience prior to the ultimate union.

iii) This transcending of intellect in the individual soul is identical with the first 'moment' of the creation of the hypostasis Intellect, the emergence of Intellect unformed before its reversion to its Principle and filling with the multiplicity of intelligible forms.

In the final stages of its ascent the soul moves from complexity to 'a simple contentment'.

iv) Risen above intellect, the soul must simply wait; the One does not look for it or reach out to it, yet has been present to it all along, and its appearance is a mystery.

i) The higher soul inhabits the Intelligible
IV 7.x

Taking it as agreed that all divine Being and authentic Reality lives a life of goodness and wisdom, we must examine next the nature of our own soul.

Let us take, not the soul that has acquired unreasoning desires and passions and admitted other affections by immersion in the body, but the soul that has discarded all these and, to the best of its powers, has no commerce with the body. Such a soul makes clear that evils are an alien accretion to the soul, and that in its purified state the noblest attributes, wisdom and all virtue, belong to it as its own. If this is the soul, when it returns to itself, it is surely of the nature that we ascribe to all divine and eternal Being. Wisdom and true virtue are godly possessions which could not be found in something mean and mortal; their possessor must be of divine nature, endowed with divine attributes by its kinship and identity of substance.

Any one of us, therefore, who attains to this state will differ little as to his soul from the gods above, and fall short of them only in being embodied; and if every man was such as this, or souls of such purity were commonly found, no one would be so sceptical, as to doubt that the soul in men is altogether immortal. As it is, we see the manifold damage done to soul in the mass of mankind, and fail to recognise it for a thing of divine and immortal nature. To determine the nature of anything we should study it in its pure condition, since all addition hinders understanding of the underlying reality.

Strip away the husk, therefore and then look; or rather, with the soul laid bare let a man observe himself, and find assurance of his immortality in contemplation of himself as part of the Intelligible and the pure. He will see an intellect that sees no object of sense nor any of these mortal things, but by its own eternity has apprehension of eternity, the entire content of the Intelligible; for it will itself have become an intelligible universe full of light, illuminated by the truth that shines from the Good – the Good that radiates truth over all intelligible forms. He will often reflect on the aptness of these words, 'Greetings, I go among you as an immortal god',[1] when he has ascended to the Divine, intent on attaining likeness to it.

If purification brings us into knowledge of the ideal, then the sciences latent within become manifest, the only true sciences. For it is not by running outside itself that the soul 'observes Moderation and Justice',[2] but in self-possessed apprehension of itself and of what it was before. It sees them established in itself like statues, cleaned of the rust of time that coated them, as living gold might shed its dross of earth that hid the gold, and denied it knowledge of its nature: how would it wonder then at its own worth, thus separated, and consider that it needs no added beauty – pre-eminent in itself, if allowed to be alone.

ii) The method of soul's ascent to Intellect

V 8.ix

Let us form a mental image of this universe, each part maintaining its identity unconfounded yet all, as far as possible gathered to a unity; so that to whatever first appears, perhaps its outer sphere, there at once succeeds the image of the sun and all the stars together, and the earth and sea and all living creatures become visible, just as they would indeed be seen within a transparent globe. Let the mind entertain the bright representation of a sphere, enclosing all creation, whether all moving or all still, or part in motion and part stationary. Keep this before you, and call up another, stripped of extension and spatial relation: abstract your mental image of matter, yet without mere reduction of size, and call upon God, who created the world of your imagining, to appear.

May he come bringing his own universe with all the gods that dwell in it, he who is one and all; and each is all, coalescing to a unity, and though different in their powers yet all, by that one manifold power, are one. Or better, the one god is all, never diminished by their multiple generation; and all are together yet each apart, but not spatially distinct nor wearing perceptible shape – for that would mean a local separation, and each could not include the whole. They do not interchange their parts, nor is each a power fragmented, its extension measured by its parts; this All is universal power, of infinite extent and infinite in potency, a god so great that all his parts are infinite. Name any place, and he is already there.

V 8.x

To the vision of that god, therefore, Zeus proceeds first, though older than all gods who own his sovereignty, and is followed by the other gods and spirits, and such souls as have the power to see. That god emerges to their sight from a place unseen, and rising above them illuminates all things and floods them with his brilliance. The lower sort are dazzled and torn away as from the sun, unable to behold him, and while others stand and look, they are disturbed to the degree of their remoteness from him.

Of those with strength to see, while all behold the god and his possessions, not all invariably attain the same vision. With concentrated gaze, one sees the source and character of Justice shedding its light, another is filled with the sight of Moderation – and not that image of the ideal that men sometimes possess, but that crowning splendour diffused through the whole expanse of the Intelligible realm. This is the final vision, for those who have beheld the many vivid forms, the gods singly and in unity, and the souls that see all things There and are sprung from that universe, themselves containing all from the beginning to the end – members of that company as far as their nature permits, and often There entire when not divided.

This, then, is the vision of Zeus and all of us who share his love and experience that higher beauty; a vision finally disclosing Beauty itself, the universal, that shines over all and so fills the dwellers There that they too take on beauty. In just this way, men climbing to high ground where the earth has a golden glow often take on that colour and reflect the ground on which they walk; but the colour that blooms There is Beauty, indeed all is colour and beauty to its depths, and the beauty no addition or mere surface bloom. Those who fail to see in full are conscious only of the surface impression, but when men are thoroughly 'drunk and filled with the nectar',[3] and the beauty permeates all their soul, they are no mere spectators. There is no longer the external contemplation of a separate object, but the clear sight of what lies within the seer – though for the most part he sees it as external, unaware that he contains it, because he looks by an act of will as at an object of vision.

Whatever is viewed as a spectacle is the object of mere external sight, and what he sees must be brought within himself, and contemplated not as separate but as himself – just as one possessed by a god, and in the grip of Phoebus or one of the Muses, might have sight of the god within, if he had power to see the god within himself.

V 8.xi

Further, any of us unable to see himself, but possessed by that God, may bring the object of his vision closer to sight, and bring himself in view, and see an image of himself, enhanced in beauty; then, discarding the image, for all its loveliness, he becomes one with himself, no separation remaining, and is now All in one by the silent presence of that God, to be with him as long as his power and his will endure. If he reverts to duality, he remains close to the

God by preserving himself in purity, and may find that same presence again by turning back to him. In the conversion there is this reward, that, though initially he perceives himself as other, yet on retreating within he possesses all, abandons perception in dread of separation, and becomes one in the Intelligible; and if he wants to see in separation, he sets himself outside.

During his apprenticeship he must keep hold of some image of the God and retain a clear conception to guide his search; and when he has learned with conviction that the realm he is to enter is a most blessed state, then he must surrender to what lies within and become, not a seer, but the object of another's vision, radiant with the thoughts that issue from the Divine.

How can one be in Beauty yet not see it? To see it as separate is not yet to be in Beauty, whereas to become it is to attain perfect identity. If sight sees what is extended, we must not use sight; only a sight identified with its object will serve, and this will be a form of self-awareness and self-knowledge which is careful not to lose the self out of desire for a wider perception.

iii) In the vision of the One, Intellect is transcended

VI 7.xxxv

The state of the soul in that moment is one of disdain even for the act of intellect, which at all other times she loved; for thinking is a movement, and soul has no wish to move. She declares that the object of her vision does not think, even though she attains the vision by becoming intellect herself, essentially intellective, and established in the intelligible realm; for although on her arrival and in her lingering there she occupies the Intelligible and is a thinking intellect, yet when she sees that God she discards all else.

It is as if someone were to enter a richly appointed house of intricate beauty, and gaze in wonder at every ornate feature, before seeing the master of the house; but at the splendid sight of him, no mere adornment but reality, and worthy object of attention, he would ignore those images and now fix his gaze on him alone. And then, as he still looks with unaverted eye and in unbroken contemplation, he no longer sees another, but his seeing and its object merge, the seen becomes identical with sight, and he forgets all else that met his eye. The analogy would be closer if it were not a man who confronted the admirer of the house, but a god, and a god not visibly manifested but filling his rapt soul.

Intellect, similarly, has an intellective power by which it observes its own constituents, and another power of beholding the Transcendent, a kind of apprehension and receptiveness such as it formerly used to see only, and in seeing acquired intellect in its developed unity. The first way of seeing belongs to Intellect when sane, but the second is Intellect in love, transported and 'drunk with the nectar', when sated with the object of desire it dissolves in contentment - and better for it to be drunk than too solemn for such drunkenness.

Does that intellect see in part, now one vision, and now the other? No, it is our explanation that makes them transitory. In reality, Intellect has the power of thought eternally, and also the power of suspending thought, and looking to the Good in another way. In its vision of him it gave birth, and knew the presence of its offspring within it; its sight of these is termed intellection, while it beholds the One by the power that precedes thought. The soul's seeing is a kind of blurring and obliterating of the intellect that remains within it, or rather, the intellect in soul sees first, and then the vision enters soul and the two become one.

The Good, spread out above them and conjoined with their union, playing over them and drawing both into unity, bestows a blessed perception and sight; and so high does he raise them that they have neither location nor habitation nor any exterior receptacle. For the Good himself is nowhere; the place of the Intelligible is in him, but he is in nothing but himself. The soul, therefore, has no movement then, because the Good does not move; nor yet is it soul, because That does not live, but transcends

Life; nor yet is it intellect, because That does not think, and it must attain likeness. It transcends even the thought of its rising above intellect.

VI 7.xxxvi

The knowledge or touching of the Good is the supreme attainment, and Plato calls it the 'greatest learning',[4] referring not to the vision of it but to the learning that precedes the vision. Instruction comes by way of analogies, negations, knowledge of its consequents, and stages of ascent; and we are guided to it by purifications, virtues, ordering of the soul, and by setting foot in the Intelligible and, established there, by feasting on its contents. Whoever attains that identity of seer and seen, and has become Being and Intellect and 'the entire Living Creature',[5] no longer beholding it externally, at this stage he is near his goal; and next is the Good, now close at hand and shedding its light over all the Intelligible. It is there that he abandons every kind of learning. He has been guided so far and established in Beauty, and until this moment is a thinking intellect; but now, swept away on the wave of Intellect itself and lifted on high by its swell, he suddenly sees – yet sees not how, for the vision fills his eyes with light, a light not the medium of sight but itself the vision.

Within the Good, there is no distinguishing the seen from the light that shows it, nor mind from its thought: only a radiance that begets these to follow it and allows them existence beside it. He is that radiance, that simply begets Intellect without spending itself in the begetting; the light remains, and Intellect comes to birth by the existence of the Good – for except from such a Principle, it could not come to be.

iv) Intellect's perception of the One

V 5.vii

Like the eye, so Intellect can veil itself from the world and concentrate its gaze within, and, though it sees nothing, it will behold a light – not an external light in some perceived object, but a solitary light, pure and self-contained, suddenly revealed within itself; and it will wonder whence it came, from without or within, and on its departure will say, 'It was within, and yet not within.'

V 5.viii

But we must not enquire whence it comes, for there is no 'whence'; it neither comes nor departs in space, but appears or does not appear. We must not, therefore, pursue it, but remain still until it appears, in readiness to receive the vision, as the eye awaits the rising of the sun; the sun which, when it appears above the horizon – 'out of Ocean', as the poets say – gives itself to our sight. But he whose image is the sun, from where will he arise? Above what horizon will he appear?

He will rise above contemplative Intellect itself, for Intellect will stand fixed in contemplation, beholding nothing but the Beautiful, and turning and surrendering its whole being to that vision; and standing as if filled with strength, it sees its own beauty take on greater radiance at his approach. He does not come as one expected, and his coming knows no arrival; he is beheld not as one who enters but as one eternally present, before even the movement of Intellect. Intellect it is which moves, and Intellect also which departs, not knowing where to rest or where he rests, he who is nowhere.

Suppose that Intellect could rest in that nowhere – not in a spatial sense; it is itself not in space but absolutely beyond space – then its vision of him would be eternal; or rather, not vision but unity, the two become one. But as it is, essentially Intellect, it must receive its passing visions by a non-intellective power within itself. And it is surely a wonder, how he is present without any coming, and how, though he is nowhere, there is yet nowhere where he is not.

REFERENCES

1. Empedocles, *Diels*, B112.
2. Plato, *Phaedrus*, 247d6.
3. Plato, *Symposium*, 203b5.
4. Plato, *Republic*, 505 a2.
5. Plato, *Timaeus*, 31 b1.

X

Mystical Union

Summary

To attain to union with the One, the soul must itself become entirely simple and formless, putting aside all awareness of intelligible realities, as before of the world of sense, and losing consciousness of self – yet in that moment discovering its true self.

The One is ever-present and within, at the centre of the soul, and the ascent is also an inward movement, felt by the soul as a return to its Father and the land of its birth.

Although Plotinus talks at times of the soul ceasing to be itself and achieving identity with the One, his dominant metaphors are those of sight, contact, likeness and conjoining, with the implication that the 'two become one' are still separate entities, as in the image of concentric circles, with coincident yet separable centres. That is to say, Plotinus' mysticism is theistic, not monistic: 'It is, that is to say, a mysticism in which the soul seeks to attain a union with the Absolute of which the best earthly analogy is the union of lovers, not a mysticism in which the soul seeks to realise itself as the Absolute.' (A.H. Armstrong 1967, p. 263)

Historically, he looks forward to the prevailing language of the Christian mystical tradition rather than towards Indian mysticism, in which Brahman, the ineffable principle of all things, and Atman, the true self, are identical.

The state of mystical union is one of perfect stillness. Plotinus once uses the word *ekstasis* to describe it, but in the sense not of frenzied rapture but of 'detachment from self', and in a context (VI 9.xi) where all the emphasis is on peace and calm. It is, however, not annihilation, but the full and undiverted satisfaction of consciousness purified, rather as the One is called 'primally Self, transcendent Self' and 'simple apprehension of itself'.

The quest of Greek philosophy for simplicity underlying diversity ends in the perfect simplicity of mystical union.

The ascent to union with the One
VI 9.vii

If because the One transcends all description you can form no conception of it, take your stand on the terms we use and contemplate from these; but look with no outward cast of thought, for it has not deserted its creation for a place apart; it is always present to those with strength to touch it. In all our experience, it is impossible to think at once more than one thought and give our mind to it; thought must be undistracted from its intended object. So here, we must realise that our thought cannot grasp the One as long as any other image remains active in the soul, and that while other sights possess and distract the soul it can take no impression of their contrary. Just as we say of matter, that it must be without qualities to be able to receive the forms of the universe, so and much more must the soul become formless if it is to harbour no impediment to its fulfilment and irradiation by the Primal nature.

To this end, you must set free your soul from all outward things and turn wholly within yourself, with no more leaning to what lies outside, and lay your mind bare of ideal forms, as before of the objects of sense, and forget even yourself, and so come within sight of that One; and after sufficient converse in its company, come and report, if you can, that communion to others. Perhaps it was because Minos attained this union that he was called in legend 'the familiar friend of Zeus',[1] and laid down his laws to be a memorial of it, inspired to law-giving by the touch of the Divine. Or a man may consider affairs of state unworthy of him, and prefer to remain always above, a likely sentiment in one who has seen much.

Plato tells us that the One 'is outside of nothing',[2] but present to all without their knowing. It is they who stray outside him, or rather outside themselves, and so cannot grasp the one they have fled, nor yet seek another when they have lost themselves. A child demented and beside itself will not know its father; but he who knows himself will know his parentage.

VI 9.viii

A soul that knows itself at other times, knows that its movement is not in a straight line, unless deflected, but that it moves naturally in a circle around its inner centre, and the centre is the point from which the circle issues; and it will move about its source, dependent on it and directed towards it, as all souls should, and as the souls of the gods for ever move in expression of their divinity. To be a god is to be bound to that centre, while what stands apart from it is man the manifold and the beast.

Is then this centre of the soul the object of our search? Or must we envisage another, in which all such centres coincide, to which the centre of our terrestrial circle bears an analogy? The soul is not a circle like the figure of geometry, but in the sense that in it and around it there exists its primal nature, that it depends on so pre-eminent a principle, and, more particularly, that souls as a whole are separated. In our present state, with part of us held down by the body, we are like a man whose feet stand in water while the rest of his body rises above the surface; and ascending in the self that is not immersed in body, we join the centre of ourselves to the centre of all things, just as the centres of the greatest circles coincide with the centre of the sphere that encompasses them – and we are at rest.

If the circles were physical and not spiritual, they would have a local relation to the centre; the centre would be a point in space around which they would revolve. But since souls are intellective, and the One transcends Intellect, we must suppose that the contact is achieved by other powers, in the way that the thinking mind is naturally united with the thought, and that the thinking intellect stands in a closer relation, by virtue of its sameness and identity, conjoined with its kin with no barrier between. Physical objects are debarred from union by their corporeal nature, but incorporeal beings are free of physical restriction, and separated not by space but by otherness and difference; so in the absence of otherness, like is co-present with like.

The One, which contains no otherness, is always present with us, and we with it whenever we escape from otherness. It does not desire us, to be attentive to us, but we desire and revolve about the One. We are always around it, but do not always look to it; just as a chorus, singing in order around its leader, may at times turn away from the sight of him, but when it turns inwards again it sings beautifully, fully attentive to him. We similarly revolve always about the One – otherwise we should meet utter dissolution and cease to exist; but we do not always look to him. But on looking to him, then we find our goal and our resting-place, and around him we dance the true dance, God-inspired, no longer discordant.

VI 9.ix

In this dance, the soul beholds the wellspring of Life, and wellspring of Intellect, the source of Being, cause of Good, and root of Soul; and these do not pour forth to his diminution, as from a thing of mass, a creator of perishable realities. They are eternal because their Source remains unchanged, not fragmented into its creation but remaining whole. They, therefore, themselves remain, like the light while the sun shines.

We are not cut off and apart, despite the intrusion and pull of our bodily nature, but we breathe and survive by the gift of the One; for he has not abandoned us, but gives on for ever, as long as he is what he is. Yet we live more completely by turning towards him, and our good is in him; while to be parted from him only diminishes us. In him the soul finds rest and release from evils, risen to a place clear of all evils; and here soul is pure thought, here beyond affections. This is soul's true life; for this present life without God is but a shadow of life, a semblance of life There – that activity of Intellect which begets gods, begets beauty, begets righteousness and begets virtue, in quiet converse with the One. These are the progeny of soul when filled with God, and this her beginning and end; her beginning, because she comes from God, her end, because God is her Good. Once ascended There, she becomes herself and what she was, life in this world of sense being a falling away, an exile, 'a shedding of wings'.[3]

That our good is There is witnessed by soul's innate love, as represented in paintings and myths by the coupling of Eros and Psyches; for soul, born of God and other than God, necessarily loves him. There, she possesses the heavenly Eros, but here the vulgar; There, soul is Aphrodite of the heavens, but here she becomes a common harlot. All soul is Aphrodite, as symbolised by the birth of Aphrodite, and Eros born with her.

Soul loves God, therefore, in her nature, and desires to be one with him, with the noble love of a maiden for a noble father. On entering this world of Becoming, she is beguiled by suitors, and deserts her Father for another, mortal love, and suffers defilement; but again, coming to hate the ravishment of this world, she cleanses herself of its affections and once more seeks her Father, there to find delight.

Those to whom this experience is unknown should make comparison with the loves of this world, considering what a precious thing it is to attain the object of one's deepest love, and remembering that these earthly loves are mortal and hurtful, mere phantoms that pass away – unlike that real love that is our Good and the object of our quest. Our true Love is There, and we may attain to union with him, sharing and truly possessing him, with no mere external and fleshly embrace. He who has seen, knows the meaning of my words: the soul then has a different life, as it draws near to him, attains its goal and partakes of him; and thus disposed, it knows the presence of the Giver of true life, and feels no more need.

We here, for our part, must put aside all else, and be set on This alone, become This alone, stripping off all our encumbrances; we must make haste to escape from here, impatient of our earthly bonds, to embrace God with all our being, that there may be no part of us that does not cling to God. There we may see God and ourself as by law revealed: ourself in splendour, filled with the light of Intellect, or rather, light itself, pure, buoyant, aerial, become - in truth, being - a god; and on fire in that state, but quenched if we should sink again.

VI 9.x

How is it that soul does not stay There? Because it has not yet escaped entire. There will be a time when the vision will be unbroken, soul no longer encumbered by body. What suffers impediment is not the part of soul that has seen, but that other, when we rest from the vision and are busy about knowledge by proof and evidence and soul's reasoning powers. The vision and the soul favoured with it are beyond reason, greater than reason, prior to reason, above reason, as also is the object of the vision.

Such is the self that we shall see in that moment of vision; indeed, such is the self in which we shall merge, perceived as simple unity. Better, perhaps, to talk not of what will see, but of what is seen, although a bolder course would be to abandon the duality of seer and seen, and count both as one. In that vision the seer does not see or distinguish, or even imagine, two; he is changed, no longer himself nor owning himself There, but belongs to God, one with him, centre joined with centre. In this world also when centres coincide, they are one, but two when parted; and this is the sense in which, in our present state, we speak of God as 'other'. The object of our sight defies description: what 'other' is there to report, when what was seen in contemplation was no other, but one with ourself?

VI 9.xi

This is the significance of that rule of our mystery religions, to reveal nothing to the uninitiated: because God cannot be made common knowledge, it forbids the disclosure of the divine nature to anyone not favoured with the sight of him. Since there were not two, but the seer was one with the seen, and therefore no seen, but achieved unity; then if he remembers who he became when he merged with the One, he will bear its image in himself. He was himself one, with no diversity in himself or his outward relations; for no movement was in him, no passion, no desire for another, once the ascent was accomplished. Nor indeed was there reason or thought, nor, if we dare say it, any trace of himself.

As if borne away, or possessed by a god, he has attained to solitude in untroubled stillness, nowhere deflected in his being and unbusied with self, utterly at rest and become very rest. He belongs no more among beauties, but has run on beyond beauty, surpassing even the choir of the virtues. He is like one who enters the inner sanctuary, leaving behind him the temple statues, which on his return from the sanctuary will be the first to meet him after the inner vision; in that holy place his converse was with no statue or image, mere representations, but with the godhead itself. And this was perhaps no object of vision, but another mode of seeing, a detachment from self, a simplification and surrender of self, a yearning for contact, and a stillness and meditation directed to adjustment; for only so may one behold what lies within the sanctuary. For one who looks otherwise, there is nothing to be seen.

These things are symbols, and wise teachers of spiritual mysteries understand from their hidden meaning how that God is seen; and a wise priest, reading the signs, may enter the sanctuary and make real the vision There. Even without entering There, if he believes this inner shrine to be a thing invisible, a Source and Principle, he will know nonetheless that by principle he sees Principle and that like has converse with like. Neglecting none of the godly gifts that soul may own even before the vision, he seeks what remains from the vision itself; and what awaits him, all things transcended, is that which precedes all.

It is not in soul's nature to touch utter non-being; even in its descent it will touch evil, and in this sense non-being, yet not absolute non-being. By the upward path it will meet not another, but its own self, and thus detached will be in nothing but itself; and to be alone and self-contained, no longer among Being, is to be in God, to become not Being, by that converse, but 'beyond Being'.[4] Whoever sees himself to be this, has attained likeness to God; let him abandon himself, pass from image to archetype, and find 'the end of his journeying'.[5]

If he falls from the vision, he shall reawaken the virtue within him, and in contemplation of his ordered perfection, again shed his burden; and through Virtue he shall rise to Intellect and Wisdom, and through Wisdom to the One.

This is the life of gods, and of the godlike and blessed among men, release from the things of this world, life without delight in the things of this world, the flight of the solitary to the Solitary.

REFERENCES

1. Homer, *Odyssey*, XIX 178–9.
2. Plato, *Parmenides*, 138 e4.
3. Plato, *Phaedrus*, 248c.
4. Plato, *Republic*, 509 b9.
5. Plato, *Republic*, 532 e3.

The Neoplatonists after Plotinus

PLOTINUS did not found a school which deferred to his authority, but his thought was preserved and developed in Rome, Athens, Alexandria and elsewhere long after his death.

His disciple Porphyry led the Roman school, publishing his edition of Plotinus' writings and his biographical essay not long before his own death at the start of the fourth century. Born at Tyre in Syria, he was a scholar of great erudition and a master of several languages; his written works were very numerous and covered a wide range of subjects. Notable among them was a long polemic against Christianity, condemned to be burned in 448 and now surviving only in fragments, in which he anticipated the methods of modern textual and historical criticism in seeking to discredit the scriptures. To the pagan Neoplatonists, the Christian revelation appealed to an unreasoning faith not grounded in philosophical demonstration; and the doctrines of the Creation, Incarnation and Resurrection implied a God subject to change, who interferes arbitrarily in the history of the world. The Plotinian universe has no history.

The pagan emperor Julian attempted to revive traditional pagan worship for a brief period in the mid-fourth century, in reaction against the new Christian orthodoxy. The theology of the revival was to be Neoplatonism, especially as represented by the work of Iamblichus, who studied with Porphyry and subsequently founded his own school in his native Syria. Iamblichus, much of whose work is lost, is thought to have been the originator of most of the developments which occurred in the metaphysics of the later Neoplatonists. An attempt to popularise the Neoplatonic faith was made by the publication of a short treatise *On the Gods and the Universe* by the emperor's friend Sallustius; but the pagan Platonism never became a mass movement or established a church. It was in the same century, however, that its doctrines exerted a major influence on Christian theology, particularly in the work of St Augustine.

At Athens, the teaching of Neoplatonism became officially accepted in the Platonic Academy during the fifth century, and is represented chiefly by Proclus (AD 412–85). The pagan tradition of the school led to its closure by Justinian in 529. The Alexandrian school, whose teachers came to embrace the Christian faith, had a longer life; the Arab conquest of the city occurred in 641, but the influence of Neoplatonism was to enter Islamic philosophy.

The three hypostases of Plotinus are developed by the Athenian school into a much more elaborate hierarchy, on the principle that to every distinction that can be made in thought there corresponds a separate level of reality. The effect is to heighten the remote and ineffable transcendence of the One, while introducing intermediary gods, accessible to human aspiration, whose influence descends to the visible world. There is less interest in the mystical union described by Plotinus, and rejection of his doctrine that our intellectual soul always remains 'above': no part of the human soul remains in direct contact with intelligible forms, for it has fallen entirely, needing redemption from beyond itself. To 'divinise' the soul the principal method is not now intellectual effort, but the magical rites of theurgy, in which Plotinus seems to have had little personal interest. Iamblichus and Proclus are not only philosophers, but priests.

Theurgic practices are advocated in the Chaldean Oracles, which together with the works of Plato, constituted the infallible scriptures of the later Neoplatonists; and they had studied at first hand the religious rituals of Egypt and the Orient. There were two main techniques for raising men to the gods or bringing down divine power into men, one involving magic tokens such as statues, stones or plants, the other using human mediums, as in modern spiritualism. A philosophical foundation was provided for such attempts to reach the gods by manipulating symbolic objects by the doctrine of the mutual interpenetration of all levels of reality; in Iamblichus' maxim, 'all things are in all things, but appropriately', and the power of the gods extends to the lowest level of creation.

Not only ritual, but also prayer and myth, interpreted symbolically, are treated with a new seriousness, and the metaphysical abstractions are identified with the gods of Greek mythology, a defensive rationalisation of the pagan tradition. It was held that a single divine name, such as Zeus, could represent different gods at different levels of the spiritual hierarchy, provided that they all mirrored the same principle. But the philosophy that inspired Christianity and Islam failed to breathe new life into the pagan gods, and the influence of the metaphysical doctrines long outlived the association with the practices of popular religion.

The following selections are chosen to illustrate the variety of literary forms in which the later Neoplatonists expressed their ideas, and some important philosophical developments in the Platonic tradition represented by Plotinus.

I

Porphyry

Summary

i) From the *Letter to Marcella.*
Towards the end of his life, Porphyry married a widow, Marcella, and during an absence from Italy, composed this letter of consolation.

In section 8, the sentiment that, though absent in body, he may be present in spirit, is more than mere words, for Porphyry recognised only the intellectual soul and held the embodied soul to be a transitory excrescence. His doctrine of the soul is discussed in St Augustine's *City of God.*

The emphasis throughout is on inner purity through virtue and philosophical understanding, and the importance attached to personal prayer is noteworthy, implying the possibility of a personal relationship with God at the level of everyday living. In Porphyry's metaphysics, there is a tendency to reduce the three hypostases to One.

The famous reference to 'faith, truth, love and hope' in section 24 reminds the Christian reader of St Paul's 'faith, hope and love'. Similar phrases are used by Iamblichus and Proclus, and their origin, for the Neoplatonists, was the Chaldean Oracles. Porphyry's faith is rationally based, not to be divorced from philosophy.

ii) An elaborate example of the allegorical interpretation of myth. Unlike Plotinus, Porphyry insists on the necessity of such interpretation, and pursues the details with great seriousness. The passage discussed is from Homer's *Odyssey*

(XIII, 102–112). The ancient poets, called *theologoi*, and ancient religious customs were treated as inspired sources of our knowledge of the gods.

In chapters 33–5, Porphyry gives a religious interpretation of the second half of the *Odyssey*, in which Odysseus, assisted by Athene, enters his palace in the disguise of a beggar and finally slays the usurping nobles.

The Cave of the Nymphs, an allegory both of the nature of reality and of the voyage of the human soul, inspired William Blake's painting *The Sea of Time and Space*.

i) Philosophic piety

8

I know well that there could be no greater trial than that which now lies before you, since you think that with me you will lose the path of salvation and its guide. But your present circumstances are not wholly beyond bearing, if you will put aside your unreasoning feeling of distress, and value your memory of the divine words by which you were initiated into the true philosophy; for a sure understanding of these words will reveal itself in action. It is deeds that give proof of our beliefs, and we must live by our faith to bear loyal witness to our teachings.

What lesson have we learned, then, from those who best understand the human state? Surely, that you must not think of me as this person who can be touched and grasped by the senses, but my true self is remote from the body, without colour and without shape, not to be touched by the hands but apprehended only by the mind. What is self-planted in us we receive from no external agency; the keynote alone is sufficient, as for a chorus, to remind us of those gifts of God that we brought with us in our wanderings.

12

Let God be present to watch and examine every action, every deed and every word. And let us consider God to be the cause of all the good that we do; but we of our own choice are responsible for evil, and God is blameless. We should therefore pray to God for blessings worthy of God, and ask what we could receive from no other. Let us pray that the fruits of toil and virtue may be ours after our labours; for the prayer of the slothful is empty words. Do not ask of God to possess what you will not keep; for no gift of God may be taken away, and he will not give except for your keeping. Whatever you will not need when released from the body, that you should despise; but strive to meet the needs of the liberated soul, and call on God to be your helper. You will need none of these things that chance often gives, only to rob you again. And do not make an untimely request, but wait until God makes plain the right desire implanted by nature within you; for in this God himself is most clearly reflected, who is not visible to the body nor to a soul corrupted and darkened by wickedness.

16

You will best know God by making your mind like to God; and likeness will be attained only by virtue, for virtue alone can draw the soul upward to its kin. After God, there is no greatness but virtue, and God is greater than virtue. It is God who upholds a man in good conduct, but an evil spirit who rules evil deeds. A wicked soul, therefore, shuns God and would deny God's providence, and utterly deserts the divine law that punishes all wickedness; whereas a wise man's soul is conformed to God, and always beholds God and keeps his company. As the sovereign takes pleasure in his subjects, so God cares for the sage and provides for him; blessed is the sage, therefore, because God watches over him. It is not the utterance of the sage that has honour with God, but his deeds: a wise man honours God even in his silence, while the fool profanes the godhead even as he prays and offers sacrifice. Only the sage, therefore, is a priest, only he is beloved by God, only he knows how to pray.

17

He who practises wisdom practises knowledge of God, not by continued prayer and sacrifice, but by practising piety towards God in his actions. No one may become pleasing in the sight of

God by the judgements of men or the empty utterances of sophists; a man must make himself pleasing to God, and attain to divinity, by assimilating his inner self to the immortal and blessed nature. And if he become impious and displeasing to God, he himself is at fault, especially through his evil opinion of God; for God, who works only good, has not wronged him. Impiety is not so much lack of reverence for the gods' statues as defining God by the opinions of the vulgar. You for your part must never entertain any unworthy conception of God's blessedness and immortality.

18

This is the chief fruit of piety, to honour the divine according to ancestral custom, not because God has need of it but because he invites us to worship him by his most venerable and blessed majesty. We suffer no harm by serving at God's altars, and to neglect them is no benefit to us. But whoever believes that the God he worships has need of him, he forgets that this is to judge himself greater than God. It is not the anger of the gods that harms us, but our ignorance of them; for anger is alien to the gods: anger arises when the will is thwarted, but God's will is never thwarted. Do not profane the Divine, therefore, by the false opinions of men; you cannot harm that blessed and eternal One, whose immortality is beyond hurt, but you can blind yourself to the perception of the highest and most potent realities.

24

No god is responsible for a man's wickedness, but the man himself by his choice. Prayer accompanied by wicked deeds is impure and therefore unacceptable to God, but if accompanied by good deeds, it is alike pure and acceptable to him.

There are four essential elements in our relationship with God: faith, truth, love, and hope. We must have faith that our only salvation is in turning towards God, and, given this faith, we must strive to the best of our power to know the truth about God; and when we know this, we must love the object of our knowledge, and, inspired with love, feed our soul on good hopes throughout our life. It is by good hopes that good men rise above the wicked.

ii) The Cave of the Nymphs

1

There is hidden meaning in Homer's cave in Ithaca, which he describes in these verses:

> At the head of the bay there is a long-leaved olive-tree, and near it a cave, enchanting and shadowy, a temple of the nymphs called naiads. In it there are mixing-bowls and storage vessels of stone; and there the bees store their honey. And there are tall looms made of stone there, where the nymphs weave garments of sea-purple, a wonder to behold; and there is a spring whose waters never fail. The cave has two doors, one towards the north for men to descend, and one that faces south for the gods; and no men enter by this, for it is a path for immortals.

2

That this tradition is not historical is proved by those who have described the island, who make no mention of a cave answering to this description there, as Cronius says; and it is obvious that Homer would have been disbelieved if he had fabricated a cave with poetic licence, and expected his idle fiction to convince people that on the land of Ithaca a man constructed paths for men and gods, or if not a human being, then it was nature herself who provided a way down for all men, and another way again for all the gods. The whole world is full of men and gods, and it is incredible that the cave of Ithaca should contain a way of descent for gods and men.

3

After these observations, Cronius says that the poet evidently intends this description to bear an allegorical or symbolic meaning, not only for philosophers but for the ordinary reader, and to force us to consider the following questions. What is the gate for men, and the gate for the gods, and what is the significance of this cave with its two doors? It is called a temple of the nymphs, and both enchanting and shadowy, yet darkness is scarcely enchanting, rather a cause for fear. Why is it not called simply a temple of the nymphs, and why the additional detail that they are 'called naiads'? What is the meaning of the mixing-bowls and storage vessels, when we are told that, instead of their customary contents, a swarm of bees store their honey there? The tall looms were set up as offerings to the nymphs: but why are they not of wood or some other material, but of stone like the storage vessels and bowls? This is obscure; but as for the nymphs' weaving garments of sea-purple on these stone looms, that is not 'a wonder to behold', but a wonder to hear. Who could belive that goddesses weave cloaks of sea-purple in a dark cave on looms of stone, especially when told that the cloth can be seen and recognised as purple? Again, it is curious that the cave has two doors, one made for men to descend, and the other for the gods, and that the way for men is said to face towards the north wind, and the way for gods towards the south. It is very puzzling that he assigned the north to men and the south to gods, rather than the east and west; for in virtually all temples the statues and entrances face towards the east, and people who enter them look westwards when standing face to face with the statues and offering prayers and worship to the gods.

4

An account full of obscurities such as these cannot be a piece of fiction meant for entertainment, nor again an accurate geographical description; the poet has an allegorical intention, and there is symbolism also in the nearby olive tree. The task of investigating and disclosing these meanings, recognised by earlier authors, we must now undertake, with their help and our own judgement.

Those who have supposed the cave and its features to be mere figments of the poet's imagination have certainly been careless in reference to the geographical evidence, in contrast to the most reliable and accurate descriptions. For Artemidorus of Ephesus, in the fifth of his eleven geographical works, writes as follows:

> From the harbour of Panormos in Kephallenia, twelve stades to the east, is the island of Ithaca, eighty-five stades in length, narrow and hilly, with a harbour named after Phorcys; the harbour has a beach where there is a cave of the nymphs, and here Odysseus is said to have been put ashore by the Phaeacians.

It cannot, therefore, be simply invented by Homer; but whether he described it as it was or made his own additions, the intention of the founders or of the poet who embellished it must still be investigated. Men of earlier days would not have dedicated temples without some symbolic meaning, nor would Homer have written such a description to no purpose. To the extent that it can be shown that the details of the cave are not the invention of Homer, but the work of those who dedicated it to the gods before Homer's day, it will be found to be an offering steeped in the wisdom of the ancients, and therefore worthy of investigation and calling for an explanation of its symbolism.

5

Men of old were right to dedicate caves and grottoes to the universe, in whole or in part, to teach us to see the earth as a symbol of the matter from which the universe is constructed; in fact, some of them simply identified matter with the earth. They represented the material universe by caves because caves are generally natural features of the earth, enclosed by a simple rock formation, hollow inside but extending outwards into the boundless earth. The universe is a natural construction of matter, and the stone and rock of the cave were symbolic of matter's inert nature and resistance to form, and its unboundedness of matter's shapelessness. Matter is also fluid, and in itself devoid of the form that gives it visible shape; and the wetness and humidity of caves, and their dark and 'shadowy' appearance, as the poet calls it, were taken to be fitting symbols of the material character of the universe.

6

It is on account of matter, therefore, that the universe is 'shadowy' and dark, and because of the intertwining and orderly arrangement of form, implied in the words 'ordered universe', that it is called beautiful and 'enchanting'. It could very appropriately be described as a cave, enchanting at first sight by its participation in forms, but shadowy if one looks into its depths and penetrates it in thought: its external and surface appearance is enchanting, but its inner depths shadowy.

10

The temple is called sacred, not to mountain or other nymphs, but to naiads, who are named after running waters. We refer especially by 'nymphs' to the powers that rule the waters or naiads, and they were referring to the whole company of souls waiting to descend and come to birth. They believed that the souls sit upon water touched by the divine breath, as Numenius says; and he adds that this is why the prophet says that the breath of God moves above the surface of the water and why the Egyptians place all their gods not on dry land but in a boat, including the Sun and all who must be known to the souls who float upon moisture before descending to their birth. For the same reason, Heraclitus says that it is a delight, and not death, for souls to become moist, and their delight is their descent into birth.

14

The stone bowls and storage vessels are very appropriate to nymphs who rule the spring that issues from the rock; and what fitter symbol could there be for souls descending to birth in the body? This is why the poet was so bold as to say that on stone they 'weave garments of sea-purple, a wonder to behold': for it is in and around the bones of the body that flesh is formed, and bones are symbolised by the stone which they resemble. The looms, therefore, are said to be of stone and no other material. The garments of sea-purple are obviously flesh formed from blood; it is from blood that purple wool comes, and from living creatures that wool is given its dye, and birth in the flesh is through blood and from blood. And the body is the tunic in which the soul is clothed, in truth 'a wonder to behold', whether you consider its construction or soul's attachment to it.

15

Why are the storage vessels filled, not with water, but with honeycombs? Homer says that in them 'the bees store their honey', meaning, clearly, that they store their food, honey being the bees' food and nourishment. Poets who tell of the gods give a variety of symbolic meanings to honey because of its many powers, including the powers of purification and preservation; for many things are preserved from decay by honey, and stubborn wounds may be healed by honey. It is also sweet to the taste, and gathered by the bees from flowers.

16

In the poems of Orpheus, Cronos is snared by Zeus with the aid of honey: filled with honey he becomes drunk and befuddled, as with wine, and falls asleep, like Poros in Plato, 'drunk with the nectar'; for as yet there was no wine. Orpheus has Night propose the strategem of the honey to Zeus, and urge him to tie him in bonds, 'when you see him beneath the lofty oaks, drunk with the product of the loud-murmuring bees'. Cronos suffers this fate, and when bound is castrated like Uranus; and the poet's hidden meaning is that divine beings take pleasure in being bound and brought down to birth, and scatter their powers like seed when dissolved in pleasure.

17

If honey stands for purification and prevention of natural corruption and the pleasure of descent into birth, it is a fitting symbol for the purity of the water ruled by the water nymphs, both for cleansing and to assist in birth. Birth is assisted by water, and this is why the bees store their food in the mixing-bowls and storage vessels: the bowls symbolise spring waters, just as in Mithraism the mixing-bowl stands for a spring, and the storage vessels for the vessels in which we draw from the springs. Springs and streams belong not only to water-nymphs, but even more fittingly to the nymphs as souls, whom the ancients called bees because they give delight. Hence the aptness of Sophocles' line about souls, 'a swarm of spirits murmurs and ascends'.

However, they did not refer to all the souls that come to birth, as bees, but only those destined to live a righteous life, and pleasing to the gods, before returning to their former home. For the bee loves to return to its home, and is a most righteous and sober creature; and for this reason wineless libations are poured in honey.

20

Homer was not content to describe the Ithacan cave as having two doors, but added that one faced north and the other south, and that the northern door was a way of descent; as to the southern door, he did not indicate whether it was a way of descent, but only that 'no men enter by this, for it is a path for immortals'.

21

We must inquire, therefore, what was the purpose of this design, if the poet's record is historical, or what his hidden meaning if the description is the work of his imagination.

We must remember that the cave is an image or symbol of the universe. Numenius and his friend Cronius say that there are two poles in the heaven, the southern at the winter solstice and the northern at the summer; and the summer solstice falls under Cancer and the winter under Capricorn. Cancer is rightly assigned to the Moon, which is closest to earth, because it is closest to us, while Capricorn is assigned to the highest and most remote of all the planets, because the southern pole is invisible.

22
The poets interpreted Cancer and Capricorn as two gates, and Plato called them two mouths; and Cancer is the gate through which souls descend, and Capricorn their path of ascent. Cancer is to the north, and for descent, and Capricorn to the south, for ascent. The north is for souls coming to birth, and it is right that the northern gate of the cave is 'for men to descend', whereas the southern opening is not for gods, but for souls ascending to the gods.

32
It remains to explain the symbolism of the olive tree planted there. This has more than one meaning, since it is said not simply to be planted nearby, but 'at the head':

> At the head of the bay there is a long-leaved olive tree, and near it a cave.

It is not by chance, as might be supposed, that it has grown like this, for it holds the riddle of the cave. Because the universe is not a random or chance phenomenon, but the creation of the divine Wisdom and Intellect, it is as a symbol of God's wisdom that the olive tree is planted next to the cave, the image of the universe. For this tree is sacred to Athene, and Athene is wisdom. The goddess was born from the head of Zeus, and the poet displays his knowledge of the gods in his apt choice of the head of the bay for its hallowed place. Its meaning is that the existence of the universe is not the result of irrational chance, but the creation of intelligence and wisdom; and while it is separated from the cave, it is set close to it upon the head of the whole expanse of the bay.

33

The olive is an evergreen which bears fruit that brings relief from ills; it gives honour to Athene, and supplies the wreath of leaves for the victorious athletes and the olive-branch for suppliants. Similarly, the universe is governed by Intellect and an eternal and everlasting Wisdom, by which the prize of victory is bestowed on life's athletes, and relief from all their labours, and from which proceeds the Artificer who sustains the universe, and lifts up the wretched and the suppliant.

34

Into this cave, then, Homer says that the man must put aside all his worldly possessions, and become naked like a beggar, and deny his body, casting off all superfluity and ignoring its perceptions; and that he has to take counsel with Athene, sitting with her beneath the olive tree, and contrive the conquest of all affections that plot against his soul. For I believe that Numenius and his followers were not wide of the mark in seeing Odysseus in Homer's *Odyssey* as a symbol of the man who passes through the temporal cycle, and is thus restored to that company who live beyond the waves of the sea of time: 'until you reach those men who know not the sea, and eat food unmixed with salt.' The ocean, the sea and their waves represent material existence in Plato also.

35

Related to this, I believe, is the name of Phorcys, after whom Homer named the harbour: 'There is a harbour of Phorcys, the old man of the sea.' It was his daughter, Thoosa, whose parentage Homer mentions at the beginning of the *Odyssey*, and whose son was the Cyclops, blinded by Odysseus. Until his arrival at his native land, therefore, he is reminded of his sins.

So it is fitting that he should sit beneath the olive tree as the god's suppliant, and by supplication appease his patron deity. He cannot expect prompt release from this life of sense that he has blinded and maimed, but is pursued for his bold deed by the avenging wrath of the gods of sea, or material existence, whom he must appease by sacrifice and the harsh rigours of the beggar's life. At times he fights against the assaults of affections, at other times he uses guile and deceit and every resource against them, until, stripped of his beggar's rags, he destroys them all. Yet not even then does he find release from his labours, but only when he forsakes the sea and forgets the works of the sea of time, and takes the oar for a winnowing-shovel, all oblivious of the sea's instruments and their works.

II

Iamblichus

Iamblichus was highly respected by the other Neoplatonists for his important innovations in the interpretation of Platonism. Most of his philosophical works are lost, but his ideas survive in the discussion by Proclus and others. (For this see Dillon, 1973).

Summary:

These extracts are from *On the Mysteries of Egypt*, written in reply to Porphyry's *Letter to Anebo*, which treats with scepticism the claim that theurgy can put men in contact with the gods or constrain the gods. Both Iamblichus and Proclus claimed to possess magic and clairvoyant powers. The philosophical defence of theurgy influenced Christian sacramental theology.

i) These chapters are remarkable for the explicit subordination of philosophy to theurgy, and also for the claim that the gods are responsive to us. The theurgist sought oracular inspiration through the manipulation of symbolic objects accompanied by occult linguistic formulas.
ii) With reference to Egyptian religion, Iamblichus reads metaphysical meaning in natural phenomena. A new-born infant seated on a lotus was a symbol of the rising Sun.
iii) This account of divine inspiration effected in a human medium by the theurgist contains resemblances to the literature of modern spiritualism, both in the physical behaviour of the medium, and in the appearance of a

'spiritual form', visible to onlookers like the 'ectoplasm' of the seance. The Greek *pneuma* is the word used of the astral body that harbours the soul. We are here a long way from Plotinus, even though it is still the intellectual soul that is held to attain to divine union.

iv) Only by divination may the soul be released from bondage to the material world and attain to union with the gods.

i) A defence of theurgy

I 15

You refer to the gods as pure intellects, knowing no declension or contact with the world of sense, and wonder whether we should pray to them. My belief is that we should pray to them and to no others. For the divine in ourselves, the unity of intellect, or the intelligible part, if you prefer to call it so, is wakened to life and made manifest in prayer, and when wakened aspires to its kin and becomes united with its own perfection. If you find it incredible that incorporeal being should hear our voice, supposing that to hear the words of our prayers the gods would need sensation – and ears, indeed, then you are deliberately ignoring that the first causes possess knowledge in perfection, and that they contain within themselves all that derives from them, holding all that exists together in a unity. It is not, therefore, by special faculties or organs of sense that the gods take in our prayers: they contain within themselves the realisation of the blessings for which we pray, and especially in answer to words hallowed among the gods and brought in union with them through sacred ritual. At such moments, the Divine literally converses with itself and shares the thoughts expressed in the prayers as its own.

II 11

You proceed to identify ignorance and delusion concerning these matters with impiety and impurity, and urge us to accept the authentic tradition; and on this there is no dispute, but universal agreement. Who would not admit that the knowledge that touches true Being is most conformable to divinity, whereas the ignorance that descends into non-being, remote from divine causality, has lost contact with the forms of reality? But you have not said enough, and I propose to add what is missing; and since you defend your position by philosophical argument, rather than by reference to the efficacy of the priestly art, I consider it necessary to give more prominence to the practice of theurgy.

Let us admit that ignorance and delusion are an offence and mark of impiety: it does not follow that appropriate offerings to the gods and ritual acts are thereby rendered false, for it is not thought that puts theurgists in contact with the gods. If it were, what would prevent the student of philosophy from enjoying the theurgic union with the gods? The truth is quite different: it is the performance of mysterious acts which surpass all understanding, duly executed in honour of the gods, and the power of unutterable symbols, intelligible to the gods alone, that effects the theurgic union. This is why it is not our thought that performs the acts; if it were, their working would be an activity of intellect, and dependent on us, but neither is the case.

It is the tokens of themselves, without thought on our part, which operate in their appropriate way, and the mysterious power of the gods, to whom they are directed, that spontaneously recognises their own images, without needing the prompting of our thought. It is contrary to nature that beings that comprehend others should be moved to act by their subordinates, or the perfect by the imperfect, or the whole by its parts. It is not, therefore, the initiative of our thinking that motivates the divine principles; our acts of thought, along with every perfection of the soul and inner purity, are preconditions and auxiliary causes, but it is the divine tokens themselves that are the principal summoners of the divine will. Thus, the divine is moved by the divine, and admits no inferior cause of its proper activity.

I have explained this at length to convince you that the full power of theurgic activity does not derive from us, and that its authentic and successful accomplishment does not depend on the correctness of our thoughts, nor its failure on our delusion. Even a knowledge of the special requirements of each type does not bring us to the reality of their operation. It may be that effective union with the gods never occurs in the absence of knowledge, yet the two are not identical: the purity of the divine state is not attained by correct knowledge, as purity of body is attained by chastity, but is a union and purifying that transcends knowledge. Nor does any other of our human attributes assist the accomplishment of the divine acts.

ii) Symbolism in nature

VII 1

I should like to explain to you the character of the theology developed by the Egyptians, who also imitate the nature of the universe and the gods' work of creation, by producing symbolic images to represent mysterious, occult and invisible meanings. Nature, in the same way, has revealed its unseen principles in visible forms, and the craftsmanship of the gods has made perceptible copies of the reality of the Forms. And so, because they know that all higher beings take delight to see their likeness in their inferiors, their wish is to complete the felicity of the gods by copying them, to the best of their powers; and they naturally produce, in an appropriate form, an initiation into divine mysteries concealed in symbols.

2

I would have you listen, therefore, to the intelligent interpretation of symbols in the thought of the Egyptians, disregarding the fanciful caricatures of symbols learned by hearsay, and raising yourself to the truth as understood by intellect.

Consider all corporeal and material existence, or the principle of nutrition and generation, and every natural form contained in matter and borne by the turbulence of matter, all that takes in the stream of temporal birth and sinks with it, or the primaeval cause and foundation of the world, the elements and all their powers: all this see symbolised by mire, for such is its nature. Yet over all this, and containing all existence within himself, there presides God, author of generation and all nature and all elemental powers: transcendent, immaterial, incorporeal, supernatural, unbegotten and indivisible, self-disclosed in his totality and self-abiding. And because he embraces all things, and gives of himself to every creature in the universe, he is revealed in them; but in that he transcends all, self-abiding in unique simplicity, he is revealed as separate, exalted, uniquely simple, and transcendent over the powers and elements of the world.

The following symbol is testimony to this truth. To be seated upon a lotus signifies superiority to mire, with which it makes no contact, symbolises the dominion of Intellect in the empyrean; for all parts of the lotus are circular, both the shapes that appear in the leaves and those in the fruit, and only this circular movement has affinity with the circular activity of Intellect, which displays its unchanging identity under a single order and principle. God himself is set apart, above the activity of this dominion, august and holy in his transcendent simplicity, and remaining in himself - which is the meaning of the sitting posture.

iii) Divine possession

III 5

There are many forms of divine possession and many ways by which the divine inspiration is effected, so that its symptoms are very varied. On the one hand, the gods, by whom we are inspired, are different gods and inspire us in different ways; on the other, the manner of possession changes and produces a different type of inspiration. Either the god possesses us, or we surrender entirely to the god, or we act in co-operation with him; and sometimes we participate in the god's power at the lowest level, sometimes mediately, and sometimes in the primal power; similarly, we may attain simply to participation, or to communion, and sometimes to union with the divine in these states of possession.

Consequently, the signs of possession are various: movements of the body or limbs, or complete stillness; harmonious sounds, choric songs and melodious voices, or their contraries; or the body is seen to rise or become enlarged or float in the air, or again contrary phenomena may occur; the voice may be consistent in volume and the pauses between utterances regular, or great irregularity may be observed; sometimes the sounds rise and fall musically, sometimes not.

6

But the most important manifestation is the descent of a spiritual form which enters the medium, and whose size and appearance are visible to the theurgist, by whom it is mysteriously commanded and controlled. The medium also sees it in the form of fire before receiving it; and sometimes it appears to all the onlookers, whether at the descent or the return of the god. And by this they come to a complete knowledge of his truth and power and order, and of what truths he can disclose and what power he can lend or wield for those who know him.

7

It is a mistake to think that possession is a movement of thought under demonic influence. In genuine possession it is not the human mind which moves, and the inspiration is not demonic but from the gods. Nor is it simply a trance, but rather an ascent and reversion to higher reality, whereas derangement and trance may also be a sign of decline to a lower level. Again, although this account may tell us something of the experiences of mediums, it misses the essential point, which is that they are wholly possessed by a god before the ensuing state of trance.

It is wrong, therefore, to attribute possession to the soul or one of its powers, to intellect or one of its powers or activities, or to physical weakness or its absence; none of these explanations is plausible. Inspiration is no work of man, nor does its efficiency depend on human nature or activities; they are merely there to be used as the god's instruments, and he accomplishes the act of divination entirely by himself, working unassisted by any movement of the soul or body.

iv) Salvation through theurgy

X 4

Only divination, therefore, in uniting us with the gods, truly enables us to share in the life of the gods, and since it participates in the foreknowledge and thought of the Divine, we ourselves may truly attain to divinity by means of it; and divination is the authentic guarantee of our good, since the blessed Intellect of the gods is replete with goods of every kind. It is not true, therefore, as you imagine, that 'those possessed of this power of divination fail to attain the blessed state in spite of their foreknowledge'; for all inspired foreknowledge is informed by the Good. Nor do they 'foresee the future, but lack understanding of how rightly to use it'; on the contrary, with their foreknowledge they receive the Good itself, and true and proper order, which tell to their advantage. For the gods give them the power to guard against the threats of nature: when it becomes necessary to display virtue and we are helped in this by the uncertainty of the future, they conceal it from us for the betterment of our soul; but when ignorance is to no advantage and it profits souls to have foreknowledge, for their salvation and raising on high, then they instill the foreknowledge of the oracles into their very being.

5

We must consider how man obtains release and liberation from the bonds of necessity and fate. There is no other way than the knowledge of the gods: for the essence of happiness is knowledge of the Good, just as the essence of evil is to forget the good and be deluded by evil. The first keeps company with divinity, while the baser portion is inseparable from mortality; the one takes the measure of intelligible realities by means of the priestly arts; the other, deflected from true principles, is preoccupied with the measure of corporeal being. The first is to know the Father, the other to stray from him and forget God the Father, the transcendent and self-caused; the one preserves true life by its raising to its Father, the other drags down primordial Man to the world of perpetual flux and movement.

The first, you should understand, is the way to blessedness: it gives to souls the intellectual fulfilment of union with the Divine. And the priestly and theurgic gift of blessedness is called the door to the divine Artificer of the universe, or the place or court of the Good: within its power, firstly, is a purity of soul far more perfect than purity of body; it also disciplines the mind to grasp and contemplate the Good, and shun all that opposes it; and finally, it brings union with the gods, the givers of blessings.

III
Proclus

Proclus (AD 412–85) was born in Constantinople, but in his youth visited Athens to study philosophy at the Academy, and later was appointed to the position of *Diadochus*, or Successor of Plato, as head of the school. He there spent the remainder of his life, dividing his time between teaching and the writing of many long, learned and subtle commentaries. The Platonism of personal exploration promoted by Plotinus has become a department of theology, with its professor and text-books.

Proclus is said to have enjoyed the special favour of Athene, goddess of Constantinople, and he practised theurgy and prayed to the Sun. His support for the worship of the Greek pagan gods led to conflict with the Christian authorities and a brief period of exile.

The philosophy of Proclus is largely a statement, in systematic and detailed form, of the ideas of his predecessors, notably his teacher Syrianus, and Iamblichus.

Summary:

i) The following extracts are taken from the *Elements of Theology*. At first sight this work, set out in a deductive series of theorems, seems remote from religious experience, but it develops concepts of far-reaching importance in the theology of the later Neoplatonists.

6 A proof of the necessary existence of *henads*, or primal unities within the first hypostasis, which form a bridge

between the wholly transcendent One and lower levels of reality. As the powers of these gods extend through all levels of creation, theology becomes the study of the nature and powers of *henads*. The gods of traditional pagan mythology are in fact identified with these logical abstractions and their lower manifestations.

23 This theorem is the solution to the problem of how higher realities, whether hypostases or forms, can be both transcendent and yet immanent at lower levels. Each has a transcendent and unitary, or 'unparticipated' aspect, and an immanent, or 'participated' aspect, divided among its participants. A long-standing problem for Platonism is solved by the multiplication of levels of reality. Thus, the One is unparticipated Unity, the *henads* participated.

57 The doctrine that, the higher the cause, the lower its effects extend, implies that the creative power of the Good is felt at all levels of creation, including matter, or 'privation', and the material universe. Evil, imagined as a wholly negative by-product of the creative process, is no longer identified with matter.

101 It is familiar from Plotinus that each hypostasis remains, proceeds, and reverts to contemplate its prior. In later Neoplatonism this becomes the basis for a further multiplication of entities: each level of reality exists under the aspects of Being, Life and Intellect. There is procession and reversion within each hypostasis.

103 The triad of Being, Life and Intellect are both distinct moments in the creative procession, and also mutually inclusive, each with its own dominant character – like the intelligible beings of Plotinus.

The general principle, that 'all things are in all things, but in each appropriately', implying a perfectly coherent universe, was often appealed to; it provided, for example, a justification for theurgic practices.

123 The later Neoplatonists came to regard the unpartici-

pated One as beyond the possibility of any knowledge whatsoever; but the *henads* and lesser deities may be known in their effects.

211 A proof that the human soul descends in its entirety, from which it follows that man's redemption cannot be achieved solely by the efforts of his own better part. The doctrine is a deliberate contradiction of Plotinus, and closer to Christian thought.

All the pagan Neoplatonists agree, however, that the soul exists eternally, and enjoys immortality in its own right as belonging to a distinct class of spiritual being. It is neither self-caused nor merely an effect of the creative process, but has the freedom to determine its mode of existence. Iamblichus and Proclus use the term 'self-constituted'.

ii) This and the following extract are from the *Platonic Theology*, a comprehensive study of the different orders of gods, making full use of hints in Plato's works.

In Platonism there are different modes of knowing corresponding to the objects of knowledge at different levels of reality. This raises the problem of how eternal and perfect gods can have knowledge of this sensible world.

Proclus' answer is that the gods' knowledge is given with their being, not externally acquired, and transcends both reason and intellect: it is a timeless knowledge of all lower levels of reality in their cause, not in themselves, and under the aspect of unity.

This conception of divine knowledge was important historically as a basis for arguing that God's omniscience is compatible with a contingent future.

iii) In Plato and Plotinus, 'faith' (*pistis*) is belief based upon sense-perception, and inferior to reasoned demonstration.

Proclus re-interprets the term and applies it to the ultimate leap of the soul, surpassing all knowledge and thought, necessary to union with the Divine. The conclusion is very explicit in ranking theurgy above philosophy as the ground of Faith.

'Accepted notions' are innate and certain convictions that men share universally, such as belief in the goodness of the gods. The doctrine was important in Stoicism.

iv) This extract is from Proclus' commentary on the first of the Platonic dialogues entitled *Alcibiades*. In modern times Plato's authorship of this discussion of Love has been doubted, but for the Neoplatonists it was an unrivalled statement of his philosophy of man.

The passage is notable, in contrast with Plotinus, for associating a divine principle of Love with the gods' work of creation, as a force for universal harmony.

Belief in *daemons* or spiritual beings intermediate between gods and men was popular, and always accepted by Platonists.

The various classes of gods referred to at the start of the chapter were identified with the deities of pagan religion – the guardians, for example, with Hestia, Athene and Ares. On the psychology of this A. J. Festugière has commented:

> How are we to explain the association, in the religious soul of Proclus, of this utterly simple piety and the search for a hidden God? The problem is an extremely interesting one for the psychology of religion. The fact is that the search for God is difficult, it is tedious, it inolves painful privations, it goes through what the mystics call 'nights', the night of the senses, the night of understanding, it ends in a God whose very essence is incomprehensible and ineffable, in short an unknown God. Now the same religious soul that aspires to this Unknown God aspires also to a more immediate contact with forms of the Divine which are more accessible, less remote. Hence, in many Christian mystics, the tender devotion to the Virgin. And I give the same interpretation, in the case of Proclus, of his tender devotion to Athene. There is nothing, I repeat, that

surprises me in that; rather, this piety seems to me natural, and the necessary complement of intellectual reflection. (*Études de philosophie grecque*, Paris 1971, 582–3.)

i) Propositions relating to the divine hypostases and the human soul

Elements of Theology 6

Every manifold consists of either unified composites or *henads*. Clearly, every constituent of a manifold cannot itself be a mere manifold, and each of its constituents a further manifold. And if not a mere manifold, it is either a unified composite or a *henad*: if a participant in unity, it is a unified composite, while if a constituent of what is primally unified, it is a *henad*. For if there is the One itself, there must be a primal participant in it which is the primally unified. And this must consist of *henads*: for if its constituents were unified they would be composite, and so on to infinity. What is primally unified, therefore, must consist of *henads*, and we find our initial proposition to be true.

23

Every unparticipated thing creates of itself the participated, and all participated substances reach up to unparticipated beings.

For the unparticipated has the status of a *monad*, as belonging to itself and no other and as separate from the participants, and it begets terms susceptible of participation. It must either remain unproductive and isolated, and so have no place of honour, or it will give of itself, and what receives it will be its participant, and its gift a participated being.

Every participated term becomes the property of a particular participant, and is secondary to what is equally present in all and has fulfilled them all from its own resource. For what is in one is not in the others; but what is present to all alike, to illuminate all, is not in any one but prior to them all. It must be either in all or in one of them or prior to all. But if it were in all it would be divided among them, and in need of a further principle to unify the divided; and all would not participate in the same principle, but each a different principle, if its unity were divided. And if it were in one only, it would no longer be a property of all, but of one.

If, therefore, it is to be common to all capable of participation, and the same for all, it must be prior to all: that is, it must be unparticipated.

57

Every cause operates prior to its effect, and creates a greater number of consequents.

For if it is a cause, it is more perfect and powerful than its consequent. In that case, it is cause of a greater number of effects: for it belongs to greater power to produce more effects, to equal power an equal number of effects, and to lesser power fewer effects; and the power which can produce greater effects in similar subjects can also produce the lesser, whereas the power capable of the lesser will not necessarily be capable of the greater. If, therefore, the cause is more powerful, it is productive of more effects than its consequent produces.

Again, the cause possesses all the powers of the consequent, and in a greater degree. For everything produced by secondary beings is even more the product of prior and more powerful causes. Whatever the consequent can produce is the product also of its cause.

And if the cause first produces the consequent, evidently its operation of producing it is prior to the consequent. Every cause, therefore, operates prior to its effect, and in conjunction with it creates further consequents.

From this it is evident that whatever is caused by Soul is caused also by Intellect, while Soul is not the cause of everything caused by Intellect; Intellect operates prior to Soul, and bestows in a greater degree whatever Soul bestows on secondary existents, and after Soul has ceased to operate Intellect sheds the light of its gifts where Soul has not bestowed itself. Even lifeless objects, in so far as they participate in form, participate in Intellect, or the creative power of Intellect.

Again, whatever is caused by Intellect is caused also by the Good; but not conversely. For even privation of form is from the Good, the cause of everything, whereas Intellect, being form, cannot create privation.

101

All that participates in intellect is preceded by unparticipated Intellect, all that participates in life by Life, and all that participates in being by Being; and of these, Being is prior to Life, and Life to Intellect.

For because in each order of existence the unparticipated is prior to the participated, there must be Intellect prior to intellective beings, Life prior to living beings, and Being prior to whatever has being. And since the cause of more numerous effects precedes the cause of fewer, Being will have the primacy among them: for Being is present to everything that has life and intellect, since whatever has life and participates in intellect necessarily exists; but not conversely, since not all existents have life and intellect. In second place is Life: for everything that participates in intellect participates in life; but not conversely, since there are many living things devoid of knowledge. Third is Intellect: for everything capable of knowledge has both life and existence.

If, therefore, Being is cause of more numerous effects, Life of fewer, and Intellect of fewer still, then Being has the primacy, followed by life and then by Intellect.

103

All things are in all things, but in each appropriately: for in Being there is life and intellect; in Life, being and intellect; and in Intellect, being and life; but all exist at one level in the mode of intellect, at another in the mode of life, and at the other in the mode of being.

Each character exists either as participant in its cause, or in its substantial self, or as participated in by its effects: in the first term, the second and third exist as in their cause; in the mediate term, the first exists as participated, the third as participant; and the third term exists by participation in its priors. In Being, therefore, Life and Intellect pre-exist: but because the character of each depends on its own substantial existence, and neither on its effects, which are distinct from it, nor by its participation in its extrinsic cause; it follows that Life and Intellect exist in Being in the mode of Being, as existential life and existential intellect; and that in Life there exist Being as participated, and Intellect by participation in its cause, and both in the mode of Life which is the substantial character of the mediate term; and that in Intellect there exist Life and Being by participation, and both in the mode of Intellect, since the being of Intellect is cognitive and its life cognition.

123

All divinity is in itself ineffable and unknowable by secondary beings, because its unity transcends existence, but it may be apprehended and known from its participants; therefore, only the First is completely unknowable, as being unparticipated.

For all rational knowledge is of what exists, and the mind that apprehends truth is a real existent: for its objects are intelligible ideas and its acts intellective. But the gods transcend all existence. Divinity, therefore, is beyond opinion, reason and intellect. For all that exists is either sensible, and therefore an object of opinion; or real Being, and therefore an object of intellection; or mediate between these, both Being and of temporal origin, and therefore an object of reason. If, then, the gods transcend existence and in substance precede what exists, there can be no opinion of them, nor knowledge of them by reason or by intellect.

But their characteristics may be reliably inferred from their dependent beings. Differences between the participants are determined by the characteristics of their principles; and participation is neither promiscuous, since there can be no conjunction without likeness, nor random, but to each cause is attached, and from each proceeds, what is akin to it.

211

Every individual soul, in its descent into temporal process, descends entire: it is not the case that part of it remains above, while part descends.

For if part of the soul remained in the Intelligible, it would be permanently intellective, either without transition of thought or transitively. But if without transition, it would be an intellect and not a part of soul, and the soul would participate immediately in Intellect; but this is impossible. And if transitively, a single substance would be constituted by the part which is permanently intellective and the part which is only sometimes intellective; but this is impossible, since they differ in kind, as has been shown. Moreover, it would be unreasonable that the highest part of the soul, if it were always perfect, should not master and perfect the other faculties.

Therefore every individual soul descends entire.

ii) The unique Knowledge of the gods

Platonic Theology, I 21

We must understand that the truth to be found in the gods transcends the truth attained by reason, in so far as this consists of multiple terms and is, in a way, confounded with its opposite, so that its existence depends on untruth. The primary elements of language are inadequate to divine truth, unless, following Socrates in the *Cratylus*, it is held that there is truth in them, but of a different kind.

Again, divine truth transcends that of the soul, as observed in opinions or even the sciences, to the extent that this admits division: it is not identical with the realities themselves, but resembles and corresponds to them, and because it is attained in movement and change, it falls short of that truth which is eternally steadfast, fixed and primary.

It also transcends the truth of intellect, which exists at the level of Being and which, while rightly said to coincide with real beings by the power of identity, is yet distinct from their essence and other than they, maintaining its separate mode of being.

Only the truth of the gods, therefore, is identical with their indivisible unity and complete intercommunion, and in virtue of this the ineffable knowledge of the gods surpasses all knowledge, and all inferior forms of knowledge acquire by participation the perfection appropriate to them. This knowledge alone comprehends all realities in an inexpressible unity, and by it the gods know all things together: universal and particular, existent and non-existent, eternal and temporal. This is not the knowledge of Intellect, which knows the particular by the universal and non-being by being; but immediate knowledge of each object, both universal and particular, even individual constituents of existence, even the infinity of future possibilities, even matter itself.

If one inquires into the nature of the gods' knowledge of all that exists under every mode of being, and into the nature of divine truth, it is ineffable and incomprehensible to human thought; only the gods can know it. For my part, I am surprised to find even among Platonists some who attribute to Intellect a knowledge of everything, including individuals, and what is contrary to nature, and evil, and who posit intelligible forms even of these. I could have much more respect for those who distinguish between Intellect and the divine Unity – for Intellect is the first creation and progeny of the gods – who attribute to Intellect universal, primal and natural causality, and to the gods the power of creating and begetting all things. For unity is everywhere, but not so the universal, and even matter, like all that exists, partakes of the One, whereas not everything participates in Intellect, or the forms and kinds of Intellect.

Only the gods, therefore, create all things, and the authentic Truth resides with them, who know all things under the aspect of unity.

It is for this reason that in their oracles, also, the gods teach us truth of every kind, universal and particular, eternal and temporal; for as they transcend both eternal and temporal realities, they comprehend within themselves the knowledge of each and all, in a single unified Truth.

iii) Faith

Platonic Theology, I 25

It is obvious, I believe, and often asserted by Plato, that it is none other than Love that draws lesser beings towards the divine Beauty and makes them conformable to it, and that is the cause both of their fulfilment and of the outpouring of divine power; it is Love, in conjunction with Beauty, that for ever unites with their priors the lower gods, the higher orders of Being and the most perfect souls.

And it is surely Truth that raises up eternal beings and sets them within the divine Wisdom, the source of Intellect's fulfilment and knowledge of Being, and of the intellective power of souls. It is through Truth that all things are filled with that authentic Wisdom, for it is Truth that enlightens every intellect and unites it with its objects, just as primal Truth draws Intellect and Intelligible into one.

But those who long for union with the Good have no more need of knowledge or activity, but to be set fast there, securely grounded and at rest. What will unite us with the Good? What will still all activity and movement? What is it that unites all divine beings with the primal and ineffable *henad* of the Good? How is it that each one of them, set within its prior as its good, proceeds to set within itself, as their cause, the orders that succeed it?

In a word, it is the Faith of the gods which, by means beyond description, brings all ranks of gods and *daemons*, and the blessed among souls, into union with the Good. For the Good must be sought not by knowledge and its imperfection, but only by surrender to the divine radiance, and by closing the eyes; only so may one attain to the unknown and mysterious *henad* of Being. This kind of Faith holds a more honoured place than knowledge and its process, not only in ourselves but among the gods themselves; and by this Faith are all the gods united, all their powers and processions converging under one form about a single centre.

To be more precise, this Faith must not be confused with the illusions caused by objects of sense, which fall short of the knowledge attained by science, and still more of the truth of Being; the Faith of the gods surpasses all knowledge, uniting lesser with primal beings in the most exalted union. Nor must the Faith which we now celebrate be identified with the conviction derived from so-called 'accepted notions'; for even if we give these priority over reason, even this knowledge is partible and quite different from union with the Divine, and a level of knowledge inferior not only to Faith but even to the simplicity of intellect. Intellect transcends all scientific knowledge, both in its primary and its secondary form.

However, we must not identify this Faith with intellectual activity, which has many facets and, being distinct from its objects, is essentially the movement of thought towards its object; the Faith of the gods must be uniform and still, perfectly anchored in the haven of the Good. Neither Beauty nor Wisdom nor any other property of Being is for all things so worthy of Faith, so secure, so indubitable, so incomprehensible to the sequential movement of thought, as is the Good. The Good is the reason why even intellect finds delight in a union more honoured than intellection, and prior to all activity; and the soul counts as nothing the rich variety of Intellect and splendour of the Forms, in comparison with the sublime transcendence of the Good. Forsaking the act of intellect, it reverts to its true nature, and eternally pursues the Good, the real object of its quest and longing; all its desire is to embrace the Good, and to this alone it surrenders without reserve.

In sum, the gods are possessed of three essential properties, which extend through all ranks of the Divine, Goodness, Wisdom and Beauty; and they have three lesser properties, also extending through all the realms of the gods, which draw their members into unity: and these are Faith, Truth and Love. By these, the whole universe is sustained and united with its primal causes – whether by the mediation of the passion of love, or inspired philosophy; or by the power of theurgy. And this last surpasses all the wisdom and science of man, since it encompasses the blessings of divination, the purificatory powers of symbolic ritual, and all the fruits of divine possession.

iv) Love

On the First Alcibiades of Plato 30

To different gods belong different properties. Some fashion the universe, give form to beings and create the order which governs them; others bestow life and generate all the various kinds of life; others, the guardians, preserve undefiled the changeless order and indissoluble coherence of things; others, exercising a different power, maintain the world in being by its participation in them.

Just so, the divine order of Love is the cause, for all realities, of their reversion towards the divine Beauty: it raises all inferior beings towards this Beauty, uniting and setting them within it, and fills with this Beauty all subsequent existence, informing them with the rays of the divine light that issues from this source. It was for this reason, I presume, that the discussion in the *Symposium* referred to Love as a 'powerful daemon',[1] because in him above all there is manifested this intermediary power, and he relates all that reverts to the cause of its reversion, the object of desire for lesser beings.

31

The whole chain of Love, therefore, extending from the source of Beauty, draws all beings towards it, invites them to share in it, and mediates between the Beloved and its aspirant lovers. It therefore exemplifies within itself the entire order of *daemons*, in that it occupies that mediate position among the gods which is allotted to *daemons*, 'between divine and mortal existence'.[2]

Since, then, the whole chain of Love fulfils this special function of mediation among the gods, we must conceive of its summit, uniform and hidden and ineffable, as set in the very first world of gods, united with the primal and intelligible Beauty, and separate from the universe of Being. Then let us fully comprehend the mediate term of its procession, shining among the gods prior to the universe: its primary manifestation is intellectual; in the second rank it acquires a directive function; and at the extremity of this order it is set apart over all mundane existence. Finally, let us observe its third level of descent, divided and multiform within the visible universe, disseminating many ranks and powers and apportioning them throughout the different parts.

32

After the unitary and primordial Principle of Love, in its threefold and self-perfected existence, there appear the multitude of loves in all their diversity: it is from that source that the choirs of angels participate in love and are filled; the companies of daemons also, filled with this god, follow the gods in their ascent to the intelligible Beauty; and legions of heroes share the rapture of the angels and *daemons* by participation in beauty. From that source all creation is awakened, rekindled and warmed again to 'Beauty's emanation'[3]; and human souls, inspired in their turn, and stirred by beauty through their kinship with the god, descend to the world of birth, to be the benefactors of less perfect souls and bring providential guidance to souls needing salvation.

For the gods and their attendants, 'while remaining in their proper modes of being',[4] are the benefactors of all lesser beings, and recall them to themselves; whereas the souls of men descend and enter this world of generation to mirror the benevolent providence of the gods.

33

For other souls, ranked beneath other gods, visit the world of mortals and the souls that live there, without suffering corruption, and bring help to less perfect souls – some by divination, some by mystic tokens, and others by divine healing. In the same way, souls that choose the life of love are stirred by the god who 'watches over beautiful boys'[5] to care for those favoured with natural beauty, and from visible beauty they ascend to the beauty of the gods, raising their beloved with them, and direct themselves and the objects of their love towards Beauty itself. And this is accomplished by that first principle, the divine Love, which unites with the beloved, which lifts up towards Beauty those who feel its power, and which implants in all things a single, indissoluble bond of mutual love, and love of Beauty.

REFERENCES

1. Plato, *Symposium*, 202 d9.
2. Plato, *Symposium*, 202 e1–2.
3. Plato, *Phaedrus*, 251 b2.
4. Plato, *Timaeus*, 42 e5–6.
5. Plato, *Phaedrus*, 265 c2–3.

The Neoplatonist Legacy